COOKING FOR
BABIES AND
TODDLERS

COOKING FOR
BABIES <u>AND</u>
TODDLERS

Nutritious, delicious and easy-to-prepare recipes
to give your child a healthy start in life

Sara Lewis

LORENZ BOOKS
LONDON · NEW YORK · SYDNEY · BATH

This edition first published in 1995 by Lorenz Books

© Anness Publishing Limited 1995

Lorenz Books is an imprint of
Anness Publishing Limited
Hermes House
88-89 Blackfriars Road
London SE1 8HA

This edition published in Canada by Book Express
a division of Raincoast Books
8680 Cambie Street, Vancouver, British Columbia V6P 6M9

ISBN 1 85967 084 9

A CIP catalogue record for this book is available
from the British Library

Publisher: Joanna Lorenz
Project Editors: Judith Simons and Emma Wish
Designer: Sue Storey
Special Photography: John Freeman
Stylist: Judy Williams
Home Economists: Sara Lewis, Jacqueline Clarke
and Petra Jackson

Typeset by MC Typeset Ltd

Printed and bound in China

3 5 7 9 10 8 6 4

ACKNOWLEDGEMENTS
• I am particularly grateful to the
Department of Health for reading and
approving the section on food for babies.
• National Dairy Council Nutrition Service
• Health Education Authority
• Dr Nigel Dickie from Heinz Baby Foods
• The British Dietetic Association
• The Health Visitors Association
• For Broadstone Communications for their
invaluable help supplying the Kenwood
equipment for recipe testing and photography
• Hand-painted china plates, bowls and
mugs from Cosmo Place Studio, 11 Cosmo
Place, London WC1N 3AP. Tel 0171 278 3374

• Tupperware for plain-coloured plastic
bowls, plates, feeder beakers and cups
• Cole and Mason for non-breakable
children's ware
• Royal Doulton for Bunnykins china
• Spode for blue and white Edwardian
Childhood china
Measurements
All cooks prefer to work in the measurements
of their choice – whether metric, imperial or
cups, but do avoid a combination of all
three. All spoon measures are level and
tested with standard measuring spoons
available from cookshops and hardware
shops.

PICTURE CREDITS
Bubbles: pages 12 br, 89 br (Jacqui Farrow);
pages 23 t, 39, 69 tr, 172 b, 175 t (Lois Joy
Thurston); page 29 t (F Rombout); page 77
(S Price); pages 88 t, 93 t (Ian West);
page 173 t (Nikki Gibbs).
Lupe Cunha: pages 12 bl, 36/37, 42, 45 t,
58, 66, 75, 172 t.
Greg Evans: page 82.
Sally and Richard Greenhill: page 64 t.
Lyons Waddell: page 61 t.
Reflections/Jennie Woodcock: pages 65 b,
68 tr, 78/79, 81, 89 cr, 99, 128, 173 b,
174 bl br.
Timothy Woodcock: pages 12 t, 175.

CONTENTS

INTRODUCTION

Although during the first few years of any baby's life, food, diet and nutrition are vitally important – to build a healthy and energetic child and to develop good eating habits that will see the infant safely through childhood – there is a real shortage of reliable, practical information on the subject.

This book aims to outline all you need to know about feeding your baby and toddler in one volume. Set out in three easy-to-use sections, the book is packed with over 200 recipes, all beautifully illustrated with colour pictures – from first purées, to tempting toddler meals then moving on to food for all the family.

In the very early days all a baby needs is milk, but as it grows so too will its nutritional needs. By four months most babies will have doubled their birth weight and will be ready to begin mini-mouthfuls of smooth purée.

Although this marks an exciting time in your baby's development it can also cause immense worry for a new parent. We all want to provide the best for our child and what better start in life than to begin laying the foundations for a healthy diet? But what do you do if your child won't eat, or just spits out those delicious spoonfuls of food that you have so lovingly prepared?

FIRST FOODS

Section one covers everything you need to know about introducing those first few spoonfuls of smooth puréed foods: including when to begin weaning, the signs to look out for, what foods to serve and when, basic equipment, plus sound nutritional advice, helpful guidelines on food preparation and masses of colourful and exciting recipes to tempt your baby.

You will almost certainly find that helpful friends, relatives, health

Below: *Section three shows how to produce separate meals from one set of ingredients.*

professionals and magazines will offer you differing and sometimes contradictory advice. Some will be genuinely useful, while some turn out to be outdated or inappropriate: the difficulty is sorting through the well-meaning confusion to find something reliable. This book has been based on information recently published by the British government in the Coma report *'Weaning and the Weaning Diet 1994'* and aims to offer helpful advice in accordance with this much-researched and authoritative document.

FOOD FOR TODDLERS

In the second section we move on to feeding an energetic toddler. By this stage your baby will probably have tripled its birth weight and will have begun to feed itself and may be developing strong likes and dislikes. Many young children go through a stage of extreme eating habits or food fads, causing immense frustration and worry for parents. Again we have included down to earth tips and practical advice on coping with a fussy eater plus lots of easy and approachable recipes to tempt your child.

Above and left: *Throughout the book you will find advice and guidance on how to overcome fads and reluctance to eat – including hundreds of exciting and fun ideas to make meals more tempting and palatable to infants of all ages.*

FAMILY MEALS

In the third section the recipes have been devised to feed the whole family from one basic set of ingredients prepared at the same time. With step by step instructions we illustrate how to mash food for your baby, make a mini-meal for your fussy toddler and how, by adding a few extra ingredients, to simultaneously transform this simple meal into something more exciting for Mum and Dad.

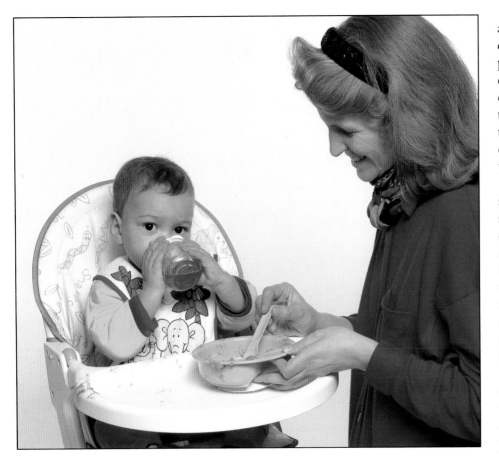

Above and below: *Start with simple vegetable purées. At about four to six months, you will find that your baby begins to take an interest in the food by themselves!*

FOOD AND YOUR CHILD

Childrens' nutritional needs are very different from our own. Forget about low fat, high fibre diets. Young children require nutrient-dense foods to meet their rapid levels of growth. Requirements for protein and energy are high in proportion to the child's size. Tiny tummies mean children are unable to eat large quantities of food while at the same time they are usually very active. Their appetites can vary enormously, but the range of foods that they will eat may also be very limited. So it is vital that the foods which are eaten contain a variety of nutrients, in combination with calories, whilst still fitting in with family meals. High fibre foods can be very filling without providing sufficient levels of protein, vitamins and minerals.

For young infants fat is the major source of dietary energy: both breast milk and infant formula contribute about 50% of energy as fat. As your child progresses to a mixed diet, the proportion of energy supplied by fat decreases and is replaced by carbohydrate. But it is important that the energy is provided by fat up to the age of two, as too much carbohydrate may be too bulky for a young infant.

Adequate energy is necessary to sustain growth. Fat is a very useful source of energy and the main source of the fat soluble vitamins, A, D, E and K, while also providing essential fatty acids that the body cannot make itself. It is best to obtain fat from foods which contain other essential nutrients, such as full-fat milk, cheese, yogurts, lean meat and small quantities of oily fish.

Try to include a portion of carbohydrate in every meal once your child is over nine months: for example bread, potatoes, rice or pasta for energy. Encourage young

Below: *Babies are easily encouraged to take pleasure in their food, however simple.*

children to eat a variety of fruit and vegetables. As with adults, try to keep salt intakes to a minimum; fried foods or very sugary foods should be discouraged and served only as a special treat.

As children approach school age they should gradually be pushed towards a diet that is lower in fat and higher in fibre, in line with the guidelines for adults.

Snacks are also important as young children require high calorie levels and cannot meet this requirement in three meals a day. Try to encourage healthy snacks such as mini ham sandwiches, cubes of cheese or wedges of apple instead of chocolate biscuits.

Obviously eating a healthy, well-balanced diet is essential for any age group, but social skills are also important. Our children learn from us and so it is also vital to eat together as a family, if not every day, then as often as possible, so that young children can discover not only how to behave at the table but also that eating is a sociable and enjoyable experience.

We do hope this book will make family meal times fun for the entire family and help to minimise any problems and anxieties you may come up against when feeding your baby and toddler.

Above and below: *Giving their child the best possible start in life is the main concern of any parent, but good food planning is easy to achieve.*

FIRST FOODS

Introducing your baby to the delights of solid food heralds the beginning of a new and exciting stage in your baby's development. Although it will be a few months yet before your baby will be able to share in family meals fully, the foods that you give your baby now are vitally important not only for their nutritional benefits but also in laying down the first foundations for a healthy diet through childhood and beyond. Start your baby with baby rice which is barely warm and only slightly thicker than milk – then move to bland vegetable purées.

Weaning from Milk Feeds to Solids

Most babies are ready to begin those first few mini-mouthfuls of puréed foods at around four months and almost all babies will be eating solid food by six months. By this age babies need the extra energy, protein, iron and other essential nutrients that are found in solids in order to help them develop and grow. Your baby will also be progressing from sucking to biting and chewing – as many breast-feeding mothers find out!

Remember that every baby has individual needs, so don't be surprised if your baby seems ready for solids earlier or later than other babies of the same age. Don't feel pressurized by friends with young babies, or helpful relatives. Be guided by your own baby.

WHAT TO LOOK OUT FOR
- if your baby still seems hungry after a milk feed
- wants feeding more frequently
- starts waking at night after some weeks of sleeping through
- shows a real interest in the foods that you are eating
- seems more restless and grizzly

If your baby is showing some or all of these signs then she is probably ready to begin solids. Check with your health visitor; a few large and very hungry babies may show these signs earlier than four months, but the majority of babies should not be given solid foods before four months as their digestive systems can't cope.

Be guided as well by any family history of allergies, eczema or asthma. Studies suggest that babies who are fed on breast or formula milk that bit longer are less likely to develop these complaints.

In the early days of weaning, your baby is not dependent on solid food

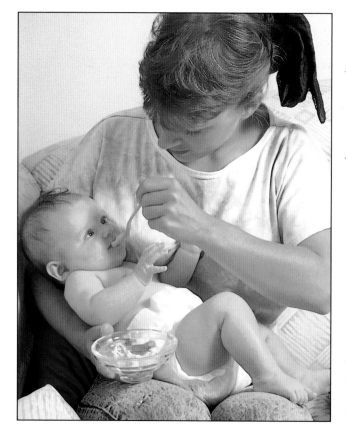

Left: *When the signs are right, start your baby with a few mouthfuls of puréed food. Your baby will feel most comfortable seated on your lap at this stage, and adopting one of the positions you have used for breast feeding will enhance security and confidence.*

Below: *If you have any doubts or worries about the right time to try purées and solids, your nurse or health visitor will be able to help.*

Above: *Your baby will very quickly take an interest in your hand and the spoon, and will play as she eats.*

for the supply of nutrients as this is still met by milk feeds. Don't worry if she only takes a taste of food – the actual experience of taking food off a spoon is the important thing. However, by six months the baby's body store of nutrients has been used up and solid foods are crucial for supplying all the vital minerals and vitamins your baby needs.

WHAT ABOUT MILK FEEDS?

During the early stages of weaning, solids are given in addition to the normal feeds of breast or formula milk. As mixed feeding continues your baby will naturally cut down on the number of milk feeds, although milk will remain an important part of a child's diet.

Up to six months your baby should be having at least four milk feeds a day and by age one your baby needs at least 1 pint/600ml whole or full-fat milk a day. Milk will still be contributing 40 per cent of the energy she uses up.

More and more health professionals are now recommending that children should not be given cows' milk as their main drink until after 12 months, due to low levels of iron and vitamins C and D. Mothers are sometimes advised to go on to fortified formula when breast feeding has finished. Small amounts

Above: *Bottles are a wonderful aid; but try to wean your baby off them by age one, or the sucking habit can be difficult to break.*

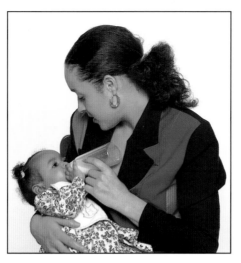

Above: *Every baby is different. There is no need to be worried if your baby seems ready for solids earlier or later than other babies.*

of cows' milk may be used in cooking from six months, but it is better to use formula milk.

Full-fat cows' milk can be given to children between one and two, while semi-skimmed milk can be gradually introduced to those over two providing the child eats well. Skimmed milk should not be given to children under five.

Only give pasteurized milk to children. UHT or long-life milk is a useful standby for holidays and travelling as it doesn't need to be refrigerated, although once opened treat as full-fat pasteurized milk.

Some people prefer to give goats' or sheeps' milk feeling it is less allergenic and offers additional nourishment, although this cannot be substantiated. Goats' milk is deficient in folic acid and must not be given to babies under six months. Boil goats' milk before use, as it may be sold unpasteurized.

WEANING FROM BREAST OR BOTTLE

You can go on breast feeding your baby, as well as giving solid food, for as long as you wish. But many mothers are quite relieved when their baby is happy to try a feeder

cup or bottle along with their lunch-time "solid" meal.

Once solids become established the number of daytime milk feeds naturally tails off with just the special morning and evening comfort feeds continuing until you and baby are ready to stop.

Whether bottle or breast and bottle feeding, try to wean your baby off the bottle completely by the age of one. Otherwise your baby may find it difficult to give the bottle up and comfort sucking on a teat can be a hard habit to break.

Once your baby can sit up and is settled into three meals a day then you can introduce a lidded feeding cup. Initially at one meal a day, then at two and so on. But do make sure to cuddle your baby while giving a drink so that the baby still enjoys the closeness and security of being with mother or father. There may be a few setbacks when your baby is teething or unwell, but be guided by your baby.

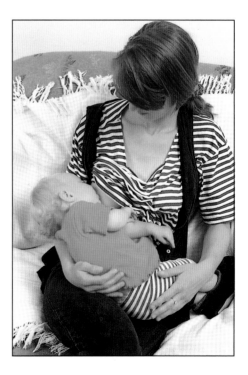

Above: *It won't all happen at once: a mixed period of feeding with breast, bottle and simple solids is perfectly natural and healthy.*

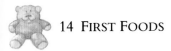

Introducing Solid Food

Many parents find that around late morning, after their baby's morning sleep, is the best time to introduce solids. Baby is happy and nicely hungry without being frantic. Offer a small milk feed to take the edge off her immediate hunger and make her feel secure, and then go on to offer solid food. Finish with the rest of the milk feed or "second side".

SITTING COMFORTABLY

In the early days sit baby on your lap, protect her with a bib and yourself with a teatowel and hold the baby tightly so she feels secure. As you and baby become more confident about feeding then you may prefer to strap her into a portable car seat or baby chair. Most babies will be unable to sit in a highchair until six months or so.

FIRST SPOONFULS

First foods should be very smooth and mild in taste. Baby rice is often the most successful because its milky taste and soft texture seem vaguely familiar to the baby. Begin by trying a teaspoonful of bought baby rice, add a little previously boiled water, expressed breast milk or formula milk as the pack directs, and mix to make a smooth runny purée, slightly thicker than milk. Test the

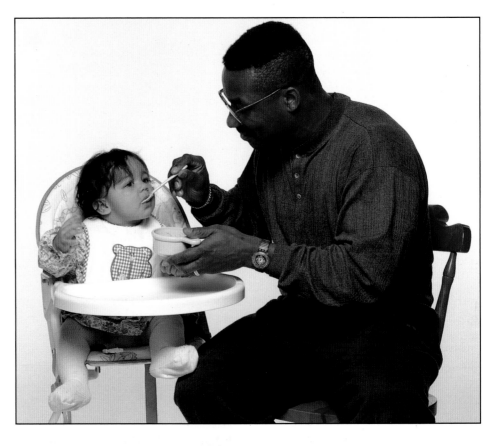

Above: *At about six months your baby will be ready to sit safely in a highchair. You should always use a strap.*

Left: *A good interim stage between lap feeding and the highchair is a baby chair on the floor, or even a portable car seat.*

Above: *First baby rice will be barely warm, and only very slightly thicker than milk.*

temperature on the edge of your lip, it should be just lukewarm – too hot and you may put baby off solids completely. Offer tiny amounts on the end of a sterilized teaspoon. Learning to eat from a spoon is quite a skill and your baby may start by spitting out the food until she has mastered the technique of taking food off the spoon and transferring it to the back of her mouth. Go at your baby's pace and don't try to hurry things. If your baby seems reluctant, then abandon the feed and go back to breast or bottle feeding. You could try solids again a few days later – there's plenty of time. Never force-feed and never add solid foods to a baby's bottle as it can lead to choking which can be dangerous.

Once your baby has accepted the idea of eating from a spoon continue with a midday meal of baby rice or

SPOON FEEDING FOR THE FIRST TIME

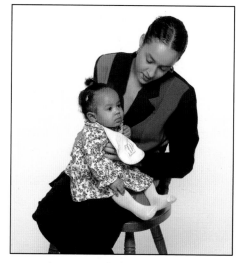

1 Sit your baby on your lap in a familiar position. Always test the temperature of the food.

2 Offer the spoon to your baby. Go slowly and if the spoon or food is rejected try again another day.

3 When your baby has taken its first solid food, sit quietly for a little while in an upright position.

puréed potato for a week or two to give her digestive system a chance to adjust to the new food.

After that, you could gradually introduce puréed carrot, parsnip and swede, or puréed dessert apple or pears. As always be guided by your baby: this is a slow process so don't try to hurry your baby if she is not ready or you will run the risk of putting her off altogether.

After three to four weeks your baby may be ready to try two mini meals a day. Increase the amount of food to 10 ml/2 tsp, even 15 ml/3 tsp if your baby seems ready. You may be able to slightly reduce the amount of formula or breast milk you use to make the purée so that it is not quite so sloppy.

If your baby likes the flavour, then offer it again for a few meals before introducing a new taste. If your baby spits out the food with obvious distaste then go back to baby rice or try mixing the new flavour with a little baby rice so that it is milder and more palatable.

Try to follow your baby's appetite and pace; most babies will stop when they have had enough. Don't be tempted to persuade your baby to finish off those last few spoonfuls.

It's a bad habit to make or encourage anyone to clear the plate if they are full. If you do it with a baby, she'll probably be sick!

Adopt a feeding schedule to suit you both. In the early days it may be easier to give baby breakfast before older children get up, or after they're at school, when the house is quieter.

Six to eight weeks into solid feeding and your baby will probably be ready for three small meals a day. But again be guided by her needs and appetite, so don't introduce a third meal until you feel she is really ready. Aim to feed your baby at roughly equal time intervals that will eventually coincide with as many family meals as possible.

TIPS
● Be guided by your baby and your health visitor.
● Sterilize all equipment before use.
● Don't force your baby if she doesn't seem ready for solids.
● Maintain milk feeds and offer plain boiled water or very diluted fruit juice as well.
● Try one taste at a time and continue with this until your baby is accustomed to it. If she doesn't like it, don't offer it for a few days.
● Remember, babies don't mind repetition, they've been living on milk for months!

Above: *Over the weeks you can build up the diet from baby rice to items like puréed carrot, parsnip, apple or pear, gradually leaving more texture as your baby seems ready.*

EQUIPMENT

Choose a small plastic spoon, preferably with a shallow bowl which is gentle on your baby's gums. Look out for packs of weaning spoons in chemists or baby-care shops. If you don't want to buy a lot of equipment straight away you may find it useful to mix small quantities of baby rice in the sterilized cap of a bottle. Alternatively, use a small china ramekin or plastic bowl. Plastic bowls with suction feet or keep-warm linings are also perfectly adequate and will be useful later on when baby gets bigger. All equipment must be sterilized first and water must be previously boiled and cooled before use.

Below: *This dish and the spoon with the shallow bowl would be the perfect starter set.*

Top left, above, left and below: *Any small dish, or even the lid off a baby's bottle, can be used for mixing and feeding so long as it is thoroughly sterilized.*

Below: *Bib*

Left: *Bowl with keep-warm lining.*

Below: *Your baby will graduate from bottles with teats to cups and beakers with tight-fitting lids. There is a variety of types, but you will find one the toddler likes.*

FEEDING TWINS

Probably the easiest way is to sit each child in their car or baby seat, side by side and offer food from one bowl. Twins can get rather frustrated if you have to keep picking up different bowls and spoons. Try to be adaptable and if you find a way that works then stick with it. Encourage finger foods slightly earlier: perhaps a tiny ham sandwich, cooked broccoli floret or carrot stick.

Wait until each child has finished their main course before offering pudding as the slow eater will be distracted and want to go on to pudding too.

Looking after twins can be exhausting so you may find serving sandwiches for lunch an easier option and this will give you a chance to eat something too. Serve a cooked main meal for tea.

DRINKS

Although your baby will need less milk for nourishment, she will still need something to drink, especially in hot weather. Always offer at least two drinks during the day along with a drink with every meal.

You can give:
● milk – breast, formula milk or, at over one year, full-fat cows' milk
● cooled boiled water
● well-diluted pure unsweetened fruit juice.

Above: *Feed twins side by side, alternating servings between the two.*

Below: *Drinks fill up the baby's tummy – so offer drinks after food.*

Above: *Dilute juices with boiled water.*

You can stop boiling the water for baby's drinks when you stop sterilizing her feeding equipment, but always make sure you give water from the mains' supply and allow the tap to run before using. Never use water from the hot tap.

If you have a water softener make sure that you use a tap connected directly to the mains' supply and independent of the water softener. Artificially softened water is not recommended as salts are added during the softening process. Check with your health visitor before giving a baby bottled water as the mineral content varies and you will need to choose a low-mineral brand such as those labelled "spring water". As a general rule, bottled water is not really necessary unless you are holidaying somewhere where it is unsafe to drink the water.

Some fruit drinks contain a lot of added sugar, so check the label for sucrose, glucose, dextrose, fructose, maltose, syrup, honey or concentrated fruit juice. If you do give concentrated drinks to your baby make sure you dilute them correctly and do not give them too often. Pure fruit juices contain no added sugar. At first, dilute them one part juice to three parts water. The amount of water can be reduced as the child matures. Offer drinks at the end of meal times once your baby is settled into three meals a day.

Never allow a baby to use a bottle of juice as a comforter or go to sleep with a bottle in his mouth as this can result in serious tooth decay.

Food Preparation

At this first stage it is vital that whatever solid food you offer should be smooth and soft in texture. Puréeing foods is very simple and there are plenty of gadgets available to make it even easier. For ease and speed, an electric liquidizer is by far the best. You may be able to buy a liquidizer attachment for your mixer or look out for a freestanding liquidizer unit. Prices vary considerably so it's worth shopping around. A food processor works well, but make sure the food is blended to a very fine purée before offering it to your baby, since processors can miss the odd lump, especially when processing small quantities. A hand-held electric multimixer is another useful gadget with the bonus of reducing washing up by mixing foods directly in the serving bowl. If you prefer to purée food by hand, then a sieve or hand mill are both perfectly adequate and are much cheaper alternatives.

Above: *There is a huge range of brand-name food processors and blenders on the market, many of which have attachments for puréeing.*

Left: *The basics – manual mashers, or a sieve – take longer but will do the job just as well.*

Above: *A purpose-designed liquidizer will make perfect purée in seconds. This is the right tool for making large batches.*

Above: *This hand-held blender takes a little longer, but the results are just as reliable. They are easy to clean and store.*

Above: *Making purée manually the old-fashioned way – with sieve and spoon – is time-consuming but highly satisfying.*

FOOD HYGIENE

Young babies can easily pick up infections so it is vitally important that all equipment is scrupulously clean before use.

● Always wash your hands before handling food or feeding equipment.

Above: *Rule one – always wash your hands before feeding your baby or handling food.*

● All items such as bottles, feeding spoons and serving bowls should be sterilized in the usual way, by boiling in a saucepan of water for 25 minutes, immersing in a container of cold water with sterilizing fluid or tablet, or by using a steam sterilizer. Larger items such as a sieve, knife, saucepan, blender or masher or plastic chopping board should be scalded with boiling water.

Above: *Scald larger objects with boiling water to sterilize.*

Right: *Always keep the surfaces around where your baby eats scrupulously clean.*

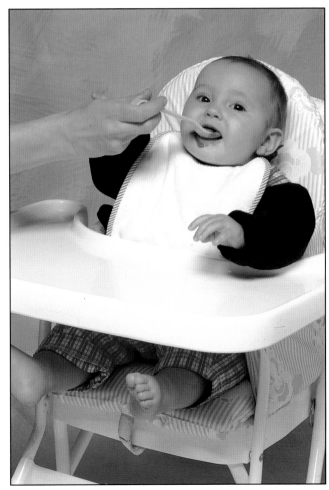

Above: *There is a wide range of sterilizing equipment to choose from. This group, all specially designed for bottles and teats, comprises two steam sterilizing units that operate electrically and a traditional container (see right) that holds the bottles efficiently in cold water sterilizing solution.*

SOLUTION STERILIZER

1 Fill the sterilizer to the required height with cold water, and add sterilizing tablets or liquid.

2 Pack the items to be sterilized into the container. Bottles will fit into the spaces provided.

3 Make sure no air gets trapped in the container – or these pockets will not be properly sterile. Push everything down with the 'float'.

4 Place the lid on and leave for the length of time specified in the instructions. Rinse everything afterwards in boiling water.

STEAM STERILIZER

1 Measure the specified amount of water in to the base of the steamer as directed in the manufacturer's instructions.

2 Pack the bottles and teats in to the container: steamers have less capacity for dishes or jugs, which will need to be boiled separately.

● Sterilize all baby equipment until she is six months; milk bottles, teats etc. should be sterilized until she goes on to a cup.

Above: *Boiling in water for 25 minutes is still the simplest method of sterilizing.*

● Never use equipment used for the family pet when preparing baby food. Keep a tin opener, fork and dish specifically for your pet and make sure other members of the family are aware of this.

● Once cooked, cover all baby food with a lid or plate and transfer to the fridge as soon as possible. Food should not be left for longer than 1½ hours at room temperature before either refrigerating or freezing.

Above: *Always cover baby food at all times – even when stored in the refrigerator.*

STERILIZING IN THE MICROWAVE

Microwave ovens are not suitable for general day-to-day sterilizing without special equipment, and many health authorities and mother and baby experts specifically recommend against using the microwave for this purpose.

However microwave sterilizing units can be purchased for sterilizing bottles, and where used, the manufacturer's instructions should be followed closely.

Right: *This purpose-designed sterilizing unit is specially made for microwave use.*

BATCH COOKING

Cooking for a tiny baby can be very frustrating. Those tiny spoonfuls of super-smooth purée so lovingly and hygienically prepared, offered with such hope and spat out so unceremoniously can leave you feeling quite indignant.

Save time by cooking several meals in advance. Freeze mini portions in ice-cube trays, great for those early days when you need only one cube for lunch and flexible enough for later weeks when your baby's appetite has grown to two or three cubes per meal.

Spoon the mixture into sterilized ice-cube trays and open freeze until solid. Press the cubes into a plastic bag, seal, label and return to the freezer. Keep batches of food in the same bag so flavours don't get muddled.

Recycle yogurt pots, cottage cheese pots with lids, small plastic boxes with lids or use disposable plastic cups and cover with clear film. Sterilize using sterilizing fluid or tablets. Cover all prepared foods and label clearly so you know what they are and when they went into the freezer.

Most foods should be used within three months if stored in a freezer at −18°C/0°F. Defrost plastic boxes in the fridge overnight. Ice cubes can be left to defrost at room temperature in a bowl or on a plate, loosely covered with clear film.

BATCH COOKING TIPS

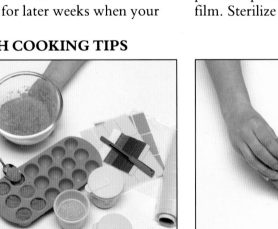

1 It is just as quick (and very much cheaper in the long run) to make a larger batch of purée as a smaller quantity for a single meal.

2 Freeze in meal-sized portions in sterilized ice-cube trays: these can later be turned out in to freezer bags for storing.

3 Make sure the bags are carefully labelled and dated. Keep only for the period specified in your freezer handbook.

STAGE 1: FIRST TASTES – AROUND FOUR MONTHS

THE FIRST SOLIDS ARE A STEPPING-STONE TO INTRODUCING YOUR BABY TO REAL FOOD SO SHE BECOMES FAMILIAR WITH ALL SORTS OF DIFFERENT TASTES AND TEXTURES.

ALTHOUGH MILK IS STILL PROVIDING YOUR BABY WITH ALL HER NUTRITIONAL NEEDS THESE EARLY FOODS WILL BE THE GROUNDS ON WHICH LATER EATING HABITS ARE BUILT, SO IT IS IMPORTANT THAT THIS IS A HAPPY, POSITIVE EXPERIENCE. IT IS IMPORTANT TO BUILD ON GOOD FOUNDATIONS.

BEGIN BY OFFERING ONLY A TEASPOONFUL OF VERY SOFT RUNNY PURÉE ONCE A DAY, GRADUALLY BUILDING TO 10–15 ML/2–3 TSP AND THEN SLOWLY ON TO TWO AND THREE MEALS A DAY.

Suitable Foods

FOODS TO INCLUDE
- baby rice mixed with water, breast or formula milk.
- mild-tasting vegetable purées – beginning with potato then going on to carrot, parsnip, or swede purée.
- mild, naturally-sweet fruit purées made with dessert apples or pears.

Apple

Pear

Swede

Carrot

Potato

Parsnip

Swede purée

Parsnip purée

Carrot purée

Pear purée

Potato purée

Dessert apple purée

Baby rice

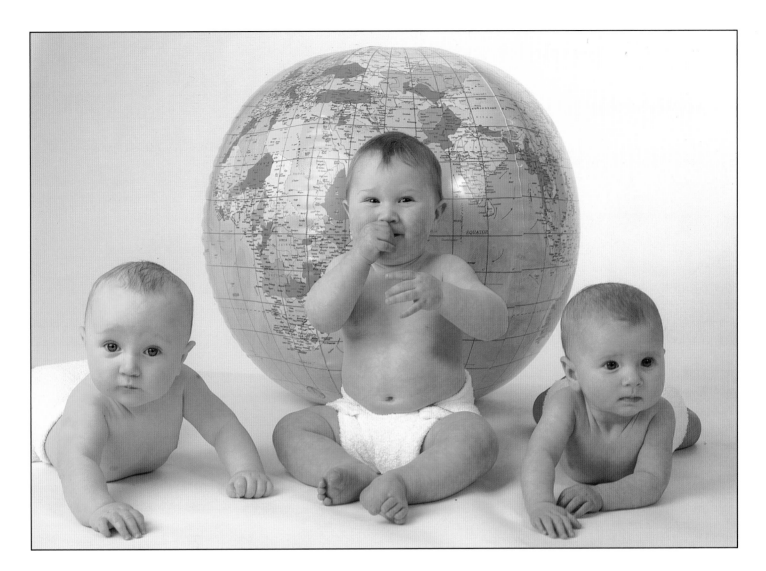

FOODS TO AVOID
- highly spiced foods
- salt as this causes the kidneys to overwork. Avoid seasoning with salt or adding stock cubes, bacon and salami to foods
- cows' milk (give breast or formula milk feeds instead)
- foods containing gluten found in wheat, oats, rye and barley (check pack labels)
- eggs
- meat, fish, poultry
- citrus fruits – can result in allergic reactions in some babies
- nuts, either whole or ground
- honey
- fatty foods

Right: *Adult favourites – but these must be avoided at this age, even as treats.*

Note: If you have a family history of allergies, your doctor or health visitor may also advise you to avoid other foods. Do check with them.

Above: *A world of foodstuffs opens up over the months: but introduce them gradually, and at the right time.*

Baby Rice

Mix 5–15ml/1–3tsp rice with cooled boiled water, breast or formula milk as the pack directs. Cool slightly and test before serving.

Left: Plain baby rice will be the staple for your baby for the first few weeks of solids – then gradually add flavour and variation.

Vegetable Purées

Makes: 175ml/6fl oz/¾ cup

1 Peel 100g/4oz potato, parsnip, carrot or swede and dice.

2 Steam over a saucepan of boiling water for 10 minutes, until soft.

3 Press through a sieve, mix with 60–75ml/4–5tbsp formula or breast milk depending on the vegetable used. Spoon a little into a bowl, test on a spoon and cool if needed. Cover the remaining purée and transfer to the fridge as soon as possible. Use within 24 hours.

● To microwave, put the vegetable or vegetables in a microwave-proof bowl with 30ml/2tbsp formula or breast milk. Cover with clear film, pierce and cook on Full Power (100%) for 4 minutes. Leave to stand for 5 minutes, then press through a sieve and mix with 30–45ml/2–3tbsp formula or breast milk. Cool and serve as above.

Right: This lovely selection of simple but satisfying vegetable purées illustrates that these bland foods need not lack colour and variation, and can be made very attractive to the infant.

Fruit Purées

Makes: 120ml/4fl oz/½ cup

1 Peel, quarter and core 1 dessert apple or 1 ripe pear.

2 Thinly slice and put in a small saucepan with 15ml/1tbsp water, formula or breast milk. Cover and simmer for 10 minutes until soft.

● **To microwave:** place the apple or pear in a microwave-proof bowl with water, formula or breast milk. Cover with clear film, pierce and cook on Full Power (100%) for 3 minutes. Leave to stand for 5 minutes then press through a sieve. Cool and serve as above.

3 Press through a sieve. Spoon a little purée into a serving bowl, test on a spoon and cool if needed. Cover, transfer to the fridge, and use within 24 hours.

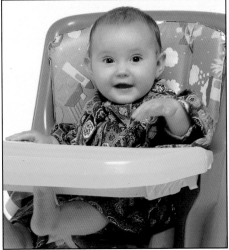

Top: *Pear (top) and apple purée will bring a smile to any baby's face (above).*

Melon purée

Strawberry purée

These tasty purées will encourage even reluctant eaters to take solids regularly.

Right: *When your baby is ready to start taking solids at around four to five months old, start with a teaspoon and build gradually to two and finally three meals a day.*

Warning: *Soft berry fruits should be introduced at around five to six months at the earliest. Do so in very small portions as some infants may have allergies and always sieve the purée carefully to remove berry pips.*

STAGE 2: AROUND FIVE TO SIX MONTHS

B Y NOW YOUR BABY MAY BE TAKING SOLIDS AT TWO OR THREE MEALS EACH DAY. INCREASE THE VARIETY OF FOODS OFFERED AND START TO COMBINE FOOD TASTES. BABY PURÉE CAN BE A SLIGHTLY THICKER COARSER TEXTURE, BUT MAKE SURE THERE ARE NO PIPS OR BONES. ALWAYS CHOOSE THE BEST, FRESHEST INGREDIENTS AND MAKE SURE UTENSILS ARE SCRUPULOUSLY CLEAN.

Suitable Foods

FOODS TO INCLUDE
- wider selection of vegetables including fresh or frozen peas, sweetcorn, cauliflower, broccoli, cabbage, spinach, celery, mushrooms, leeks
- poultry
- mild tasting fresh or frozen fish – plaice, cod, haddock, trout
- small quantities of very lean red meat
- small quantities of split pulses – peas, red lentils and very well cooked or canned whole pulses – chick-peas, beans
- more interesting fruits – banana, apricots, peaches, plums, strawberries, raspberries, melon (Warning: offer tiny amounts of soft berry fruits as some children may be allergic to them.)
- gluten-free cereals – rice, cornflour
- small quantities of cocoa

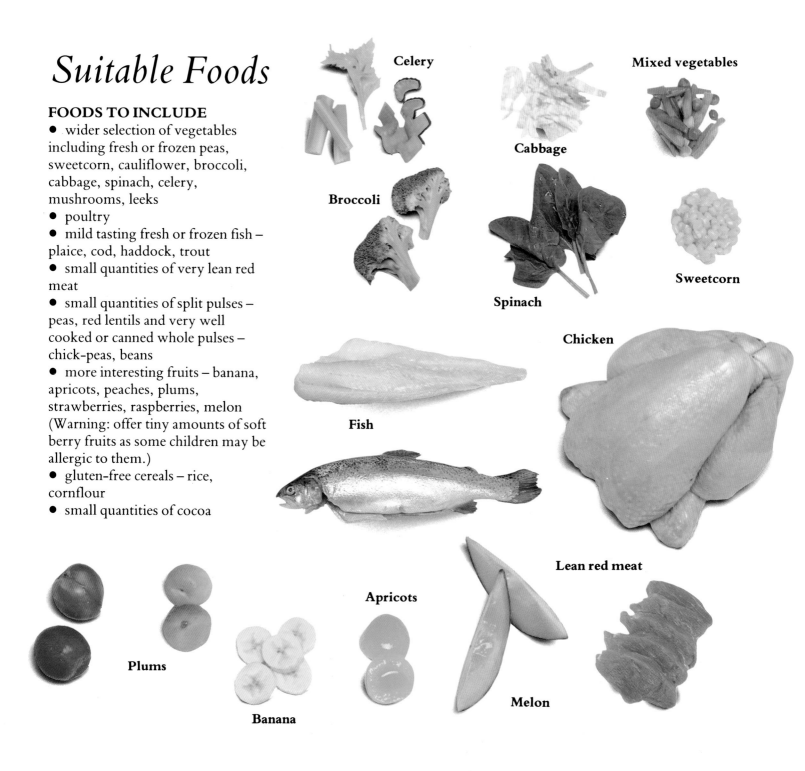

Celery

Mixed vegetables

Cabbage

Broccoli

Spinach

Sweetcorn

Chicken

Fish

Lean red meat

Plums

Banana

Apricots

Melon

Above: *Every day brings a new taste: these young gourmets can't wait!*

FOODS TO AVOID
- gluten-based cereals, wheat flour and bread
- cows' milk and milk products
- eggs
- citrus fruit
- nuts, ground or whole
- fatty foods
- chillies and highly spiced foods

Below: *Even super-healthy adult foods such as wholewheat bread and oranges should still be avoided at this stage.*

Chick-peas

Cocoa

Split peas

Cornflour

Lentils

Rice

Reheating, Freezing and Using a Microwave

REHEATING BABY FOOD

Reheating food sounds straightforward but it is vitally important that these rules are followed as tepid food provides the perfect breeding ground for bacteria, especially if left uncovered in a warm kitchen and reheated several times.

- Don't reheat food more than once. It is a health risk, and can be dangerous.

- If you have a large batch of baby food then reheat just a portion in a saucepan and leave the remaining mixture in a covered bowl in the fridge. If your baby is still hungry then reheat a little extra again with the remaining mixture left in the fridge.

- Reheat small quantities of baby food in a sterilized heat-proof container, covered with a saucer or small plate and put into a small saucepan half filled with boiling water. Or spoon larger quantities straight into a saucepan, cover and bring to the boil.

- Make sure food is piping hot all the way through to kill any bacteria. Food should be 70°C/158°F for a minimum of 2 minutes. Take off the heat and allow to cool. Test before serving to baby.

REHEATING TIPS

1 Reheat small quantities in a sterilized bowl, covered with a dish or silver foil.

2 Place the bowl into a pan half filled with boiling water. Make sure the food is cooked through.

3 For larger quantities, put the food straight into the pan and bring to the boil.

FREEZING

When using a freezer for storing homemade baby foods, use up the foods as soon as possible as the texture preferred by the child will change very quickly as the child develops.

Keeping a well-stocked freezer of basic stores can be a lifesaver: there is nothing worse than going shopping with little children, especially when they're tired and freezing will save you trip after trip.

Make sure to always label foods so you know exactly when they went into the freezer and double check against this handy list of storage dates:

Meat and poultry
Beef and lamb	4–6 months
Pork and veal	4–6 months
Minced beef	3–4 months
Sausages and sausagemeat	2–3 months
Ham and bacon joints	3–4 months
Chicken and turkey	10–12 months
Duck and goose	4–6 months

Fish
White fish	6–8 months
Oily fish	3–4 months
Fish portions	3–4 months
Shellfish	2–3 months

Fruit and vegetables
Fruit with or without sugar	8–10 months
Fruit juices	4–6 months
Most vegetables	10–12 months
Mushrooms and tomatoes	6–8 months

Dairy produce
Cream	6–8 months
Butter, unsalted	6–8 months
Butter, salted	3–4 months
Cheese, hard	4–6 months
Cheese, soft	3–4 months
Ice cream	3–4 months

Prepared foods
Ready prepared meals, highly seasoned	2–3 months
Ready prepared meals, average seasoning	4–6 months
Cakes	4–6 months
Bread, all kinds	2–3 months
Other yeast products and pastries	3–4 months

* Chart published by kind permission of the Food Safety Advisory Centre

USING A MICROWAVE

Health advisers do not recommend using a microwave for reheating as the food heats up unevenly but if you decide to microwave baby food then make sure you stir the food thoroughly after cooking. Leave the dish to stand for 2–3 minutes before stirring again so that "hot spots" are well stirred into the mixture, and always check the temperature before serving. Choose the type of dish carefully as some pottery dishes can get very hot; plastic or pyrex dishes are the most successful in the microwave, heating food quickly but staying relatively cool themselves.

Top: *All parents will find the microwave incredibly helpful and time-saving. It can be used for heating milk and drinks (for toddlers – not newborns), for defrosting, reheating and cooking prepared foods.*

1 Cover the dish with clear film, pierce and place in the oven.

2 When cooked, remove and stir.

MICROWAVING TIPS

● Never warm milk for a new born or young baby in the microwave.

● For older children warm milk in a bottle without the teet or an uncovered feeder beaker for 30–45 seconds. Stir well and always test the temperature of the milk (*not* the temperature of the container) before serving to make sure that the milk is an even and comfortable temperature. Do also seek advice from your health visitor.

● To defrost ice cubes of baby food, press three into a baby dish, cover with clear film and thaw in the microwave on Defrost (30%) setting for 1 to 2 minutes. Stir well then re-cover and microwave on Full Power (100%) for 1 minute. Stir well to avoid hot spots then test the temperature.

Autumn Harvest

Makes: 600ml/1 pint/2½ cups

115g/4oz carrot
115g/4oz parsnip
115g/4oz swede
115g/4oz potato
300ml/½ pint/1¼ cups formula milk

5 Cover the remaining food and transfer to the fridge as soon as possible. Use within 24 hours.

- Suitable for freezing.

4 Spoon a little into a bowl. Test the temperature and cool if necessary, before giving to baby.

TIP
Thin the purée down with a little extra formula milk if your baby prefers a very soft purée.

1 Trim and peel the carrot, parsnip, swede and potato and place in a colander. Rinse under cold water, drain and chop.

2 Place the chopped vegetables in a saucepan with the formula milk then bring to the boil, cover and simmer for 20 minutes or until they are very soft.

3 Purée or sieve the vegetables until they are smooth.

Mixed Vegetable Platter

Makes: 600ml/1 pint/2½ cups

115g/4oz carrot
175g/6oz potato
115g/4oz broccoli
50g/2oz green cabbage
300ml/½ pint/1¼ cups formula milk

1 Peel the carrot and potato, rinse, chop and place in a saucepan. Wash the broccoli and cabbage and cut the broccoli into florets, the stems into slices and shred the cabbage finely.

2 Add the milk to the carrot and potato, bring to the boil then cover and simmer for 10 minutes.

3 Add the broccoli stems and florets and cabbage and cook, covered, for 10 minutes until all the vegetables are tender.

4 Purée or sieve the vegetables until smooth.

5 Spoon a little into a bowl. Test the temperature and cool if necessary, before giving to baby.

6 Cover the remaining food and transfer to the fridge as soon as possible. Use within 24 hours.

● Suitable for freezing.

Carrot, Lentil and Coriander Purée

Makes: 600ml/1 pint/2½ cups

| 350g/12oz carrots |
| 175g/6oz potato |
| 50g/2oz/¼ cup red lentils |
| 2.5ml/½ tsp ground coriander |
| 300ml/½ pint/1¼ cups formula milk |

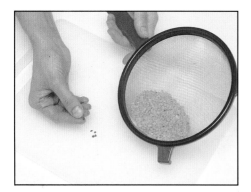

1 Trim and peel the carrots and potatoes and then chop into small cubes and place in a saucepan. Rinse the lentils thoroughly, discarding any black bits.

2 Add the lentils, coriander and milk to the pan and bring to the boil, then cover and simmer for 40 minutes, until the lentils are very soft. Top up with a little extra boiling water if necessary.

TIP
The mixture thickens on cooling so any remaining mixture will need to be thinned slightly with a little formula milk before reheating for the next meal.

3 Purée or sieve the vegetable and lentil mixture until smooth.

4 Spoon a little into a bowl. Test the temperature and cool if necessary, before giving to baby.

5 Cover the remaining purée and transfer to the fridge as soon as possible. Use within 24 hours.

● Suitable for freezing.

Red Pepper Risotto

Makes: 600ml/1 pint/2½ cups

50g/2oz/¼ cup long grain rice

300ml/½ pint/1¼ cups formula milk

75g/3oz red pepper

75g/3oz courgette

50g/2oz celery

1 Place the rice and milk in a saucepan, bring to the boil and simmer, uncovered, for 5 minutes.

2 Discard the core and seeds from the pepper and trim the courgette and celery. Place the vegetables in a colander and rinse under cold water then chop them into small pieces.

3 Add the vegetables to the rice mixture, bring to the boil, cover and simmer for about 10 minutes or until the rice is soft.

● Suitable for freezing.

4 Purée or sieve the rice and vegetable mixture until smooth.

5 Spoon a little into a bowl. Test the temperature and cool if necessary, before giving to baby.

6 Cover the remaining food and transfer to the fridge as soon as possible. Use within 24 hours.

Parsnip and Broccoli Mix

Makes: 600ml/1 pint/2½ cups

225g/8oz parsnips

115g/4oz broccoli

300ml/½ pint/1¼ cups formula milk

1 Trim and peel the parsnips and place in a colander with the broccoli. Rinse the parsnips and broccoli under cold water. Chop the parsnips and cut the broccoli into florets, slicing the stems.

2 Put the parsnips in a saucepan with the milk, bring to the boil, then cover and simmer for about 10 minutes.

3 Add the broccoli and simmer for a further 10 minutes, until the vegetables are soft.

4 Purée or sieve the vegetable mixture to make a completely smooth purée.

5 Spoon a little into a bowl. Test the temperature and cool if necessary, before giving to baby.

6 Cover the remaining purée and transfer to the fridge as soon as possible. Use within 24 hours.

● Suitable for freezing.

Turkey Stew with Carrots and Sweetcorn

Makes: 600ml/1 pint/2½ cups

175g/6oz potato
175g/6oz carrot
115g/4oz turkey breast, skinned and boned
50g/2oz/⅓ cup frozen sweetcorn
300ml/½ pint/1¼ cups formula milk

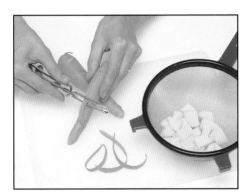

1 Trim and peel the potato and carrots, rinse under cold water and then chop into small cubes.

2 Rinse the turkey and cut into thin strips. Place in a small saucepan with the potato and carrot.

3 Add the sweetcorn and milk. Cover and simmer for 20 minutes, until the turkey is cooked. Purée or sieve the mixture until completely smooth.

4 Spoon a little into a bowl. Test the temperature and cool if necessary, before giving to baby.

5 Cover the remaining food and refrigerate. Use within 24 hours.

• Suitable for freezing.

TIP
Bring the mixture to the boil in a flameproof casserole and transfer to a preheated oven 180°C/350°F/ Gas 4 and cook for 1¼ hours if preferred.

Chicken and Parsnip Purée

Makes: 600ml/1 pint/2½ cups

350g/12oz parsnips

115g/4oz chicken breast, skinned and boned

300ml/½ pint/1¼ cups formula milk

1 Peel the parsnips, and trim the woody tops and bottoms. Rinse and chop roughly.

2 Rinse the chicken under cold water and cut into small pieces.

3 Place the parsnips, chicken and milk in a saucepan. Cover and simmer for 20 minutes or until the parsnips are tender.

4 Purée or sieve the chicken and parsnip mixture until smooth.

5 Spoon into a bowl. Test the temperature and cool if necessary, before giving to baby.

6 Cover the remaining purée and transfer to the fridge as soon as possible. Use within 24 hours.

● Suitable for freezing.

TIP
For a very smooth purée, drain all the liquid into a liquidizer and add half the solids, blend until smooth then add the remaining ingredients. If using a food processor, add all the solids and a little liquid, process until smooth then add the remaining liquid.

Cock-a-Leekie Casserole

Makes: 600ml/1 pint/2½ cups

50g/2oz leek

275g/10oz potatoes

115g/4oz chicken breast, skinned and boned

300ml/½ pint/1¼ cups formula milk

1 Halve the leek lengthways and rinse under running water to remove any dirt or grit.

2 Peel potatoes and cut into small dice. Rinse the chicken and cut into pieces and thinly slice the leek.

3 Place the vegetables and chicken in a saucepan with the milk.

4 Bring the mixture to the boil, cover with a lid and simmer gently for 20 minutes, until the potatoes are just tender. Purée or sieve the mixture until it is completely smooth.

TIP
You can vary the texture of this recipe depending on how you purée the mixture. A fine sieve produces the finest consistency, then a food processor, while a food mill gives the coarsest texture. Starchy vegetables thicken and bind the purée together. Any root vegetable can be used for this recipe, but make sure it is thoroughly cooked before blending.

5 Spoon a little into a bowl. Test the temperature and cool if necessary, before giving to baby. Use within 24 hours.

• Suitable for freezing.

Trout and Courgette Savoury

Makes: 600ml/1 pint/2½ cups

275g/10oz potatoes
175g/6oz courgettes
115g/4oz pink trout fillet
250ml/8fl oz/1 cup formula milk

1 Peel the potatoes, trim the courgettes and rinse under cold water. Dice the potatoes and cut the courgettes into slices.

2 Place the vegetables in a saucepan. Rinse the trout and arrange on top, then pour over the milk. Bring to the boil, cover and simmer for 15 minutes, until the potatoes and fish are cooked.

3 Lift the trout out of the pan and peel off the skin. Break it into pieces with a knife and fork, checking carefully for any bones.

4 Purée or sieve the fish, the vegetables and the liquid until quite smooth.

5 Spoon a little into a bowl. Test the temperature and cool if necessary, before giving to baby.

6 Cover any remaining food and transfer to the fridge as soon as possible. Use within 24 hours.

• Suitable for freezing.

Fisherman's Pie

Makes: 600ml/1 pint/2½ cups

350g/12oz potatoes

90g/3½oz brick frozen skinless cod

25g/1oz/¼ cup frozen peas

25g/1oz/2 tbsp frozen sweetcorn

300ml/½ pint/1¼ cups formula milk

1 Peel and rinse the potatoes and cut into even-sized pieces. Place in a saucepan with the fish, peas, sweetcorn and milk.

2 Bring to the boil, cover and simmer for 15 minutes until the potatoes are very tender.

3 Lift the fish out of the pan and break into pieces with a knife and fork, checking carefully and removing any small bones.

4 Purée or sieve fish, vegetables and cooking liquid until completely smooth.

5 Spoon a little into a bowl. Test the temperature and cool if necessary, before giving to baby.

6 Cover the remaining purée and place in the fridge as soon as possible. Use within 24 hours.

● Suitable for freezing.

Apple Ambrosia

Makes: 300ml/½ pint/1¼ cups

1 dessert apple

25g/1oz flaked rice

300ml/½ pint/1¼ cups formula milk

1 Quarter, core and peel the apple. Slice thinly and place in a saucepan with the rice and milk.

2 Bring to the boil then simmer over a gentle heat for 10–12 minutes until the rice is soft, stirring occasionally with a wooden spoon.

3 Purée the apple and rice mixture until completely smooth.

4 Spoon into a bowl. Test the temperature and cool if necessary, before giving to baby. Cover the remaining purée and transfer to the fridge as soon as possible. Use within 24 hours.

VARIATION
Chocolate Pudding
Cook the rice as above but without the apple. Stir 25g/1oz milk chocolate dots and 15ml/1tbsp caster sugar into the hot rice and then purée until smooth. Spoon into small dishes and cool as necessary.

Fruit Salad Purée

Makes: 350ml/12fl oz/1½ cups

1 nectarine or peach

1 dessert apple

1 ripe pear

25g/1oz fresh or frozen raspberries
   or strawberries

1 Halve the nectarine or peach, discard the stone then peel and chop. Peel, quarter and core the apple and pear and slice thinly.

2 Put the prepared fruits, the hulled raspberries or strawberries and 15ml/1 tbsp water in a saucepan. Cover and simmer for 10 minutes until the fruit is soft.

3 Press the mixture through a sieve or process and then sieve to remove the berry pips. Discard the pips.

4 Spoon a little into a baby bowl. Test the temperature and cool if necessary, before giving to baby.

5 Cover the remaining purée and transfer to the fridge as soon as possible. Use within 24 hours.

● Suitable for freezing.

> **TIP**
> Babies tend to eat smaller quantities of dessert so it is best to open freeze purée in a sterilized ice cube tray. Transfer the cubes to a plastic bag once frozen.

VARIATION
Peach and Melon Blush
To make 175ml/6 fl oz/¾ cup, take 1 ripe peach and ¼ ripe charentais melon. Peel and halve the peach, discard the stone and cut up the fruit. Scoop the seeds out of the melon and cut away the skin. Roughly chop the melon into pieces.

   Purée or sieve the fruit until completely smooth. Spoon a little into a bowl and serve.

STAGE 3: SIX TO NINE MONTHS

Baby purée can be processed or mashed but still needs to be fairly soft. A few small bits can be introduced, but be guided by your baby and adjust the textures as required. As always, don't rush things and go at your baby's pace.

If liked, let your baby hold a second spoon while you are feeding her to help develop co-ordination. This is the first step towards self-feeding.

All the recipes from the previous section can still be made for your growing baby; just adjust the texture so that foods are slightly coarser.

Suitable Foods

FOODS TO INCLUDE
- wheat-based foods, pasta, bread – first fingers of toast or bread sticks
- breakfast cereals such as Ready Brek or Weetabix made up with cows' milk
- cows' milk and dairy foods, e.g. yogurt, cottage cheese, mild Cheddar and Edam cheese
- red meat, but make sure you trim off fat and gristle
- hard-boiled egg yolk
- citrus fruits
- fingers of cooked carrot, broccoli
- smooth peanut butter

Breakfast cereals

Mild cheeses

Yogurt

Lean red meat

Cottage cheese

Bread

Fish

Pasta

Citrus fruit

Cooked egg yolk

Peanut butter

Broccoli and carrot

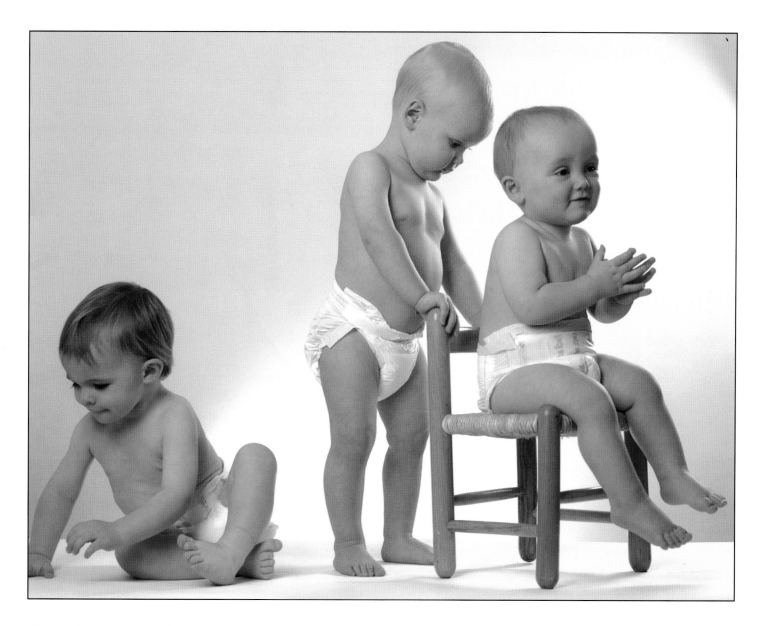

Above: *At six to nine months your baby will be delighted to try pasta and cheese.*

FOODS TO AVOID
- egg white
- whole or chopped nuts
- canned fish in brine
- organ meats – liver, kidney
- chillies and other very spicy foods
- salty foods
- sugary foods

Right: *There is still a wide range of fatty, salty and spicy foods that must be avoided.*

Choosing a Highchair

There is a surprisingly wide choice of highchairs available in a range of finishes, colours and price levels so make sure you shop around before you buy.

Three-in-one type

CONVERTIBLE CHAIRS

Designed for babies between four weeks and six months, these chairs can convert from a highchair into a swing and some models into a baby chair and rocker too. It is best to buy one of these when the baby is very young so that you get maximum use from it. The only disadvantage may be the space required for the frame. The ease in converting from one type of chair to another varies from model to model, so you would be well advised to practise in the shop before buying. Most chairs have white painted frames.

THREE-IN-ONE CHAIRS

Various designs on the market convert into a separate chair, chair and table or highchair. Some simply clip apart while others require a little help with a screwdriver. There are good rigid structures available with a wide range of decorative seat patterns. They are available in wood or white finishes. The low chair is suitable for children up to four years old if used without the tray.

Elevator type

ELEVATOR CHAIRS

These slightly more expensive chairs convert from a highchair to a low chair. Some models have adjustable tray settings to fit a growing child. The frames are mostly available in white metal, with attractive seating.

TIPS
● For maximum use of a highchair, buy a booster cushion for the early days when your baby first begins to use the chair. Adjust the tray position as well, if possible.
● Check that the highchair is easy to clean – dried-on rusk can be impossible to clean off. Look out for possible dirt traps on the seat or around the tray fixing.
● Make sure that the chair is sturdy and rigid – it will need to withstand considerable wear.

Above: *A portable clip-on chair.*

● If using a clip-on highchair make sure that the table is suitable and will be able to withstand the weight of your child. Never, in any circumstances, fix on to glass.

FOLDING CHAIRS

These less expensive chairs, available in wood or white finishes, usually fold up in a scissor movement. Some can be folded crossways for packing into the boot of the car. Before buying, check how easy they are to fold out and up and make sure the frame is rigid when opened out.

Folding type

COUNTRY-TYPE CHAIRS

These are sturdy wooden highchairs usually with a wooden tray and attractive cottage-style spindle features. The seat can be hard for baby so it is best to buy a fitted chair cushion.

PORTABLE CHAIRS

There are two main types available:
● a very simple cloth tie, useful for visiting friends or eating out as it will fold up and fit in a bag. However, it is not really suitable for everyday use as the child is literally tied on to the chair and so cannot reach the table to feed himself.
● clip-on seats where the frames are placed under and over the edge of a dining table. Check that the table is strong enough and is not likely to overbalance before you put your baby in the chair.

1 Undo the tray catches by pressing both sides at once, and fold the tray upwards.

2 Undo the side catches which keep the frame rigid so the chair can scissor in two.

3 This allows you to fold the chair over on to itself: the design is incredibly neat and compact.

4 It is now ready for storing, putting out of the way, or popping in to the boot of the car.

TIPS
● Always use a safety harness. Although most highchairs have a three point lap strap you will probably have to buy straps that will go around your baby's body and clip on to the chair. It is amazing how quickly a baby learns to wriggle out of a highchair when you're not looking.
● Never leave a child in a highchair unattended.

Above: *Always strap your baby in tightly*.

Shepherd's Pie

Makes: 600ml/1 pint/2½ cups

2 tomatoes
¼ onion
225g/8oz potato
50g/2oz button mushrooms
115g/4oz lean minced beef
250ml/8fl oz/1 cup water
15ml/1 tbsp tomato ketchup
pinch of dried mixed herbs

4 Add the tomatoes, potato, mushrooms and onion and cook for a further 3 minutes. Stir well to blend all the flavours together.

5 Add the water, ketchup and herbs. Bring to the boil then reduce the heat, cover and simmer for 40 minutes until the meat and vegetables are tender.

6 Process or mash the meat and vegetables just enough to give the desired consistency.

7 Spoon a little into a bowl. Test the temperature and cool if necessary, before giving to baby.

8 Cover the remainder and refrigerate. Use within 24 hours.

1 Make a cross cut in each tomato, put in a small bowl and cover with boiling water. Leave to stand for 1 minute and then drain and peel off the skins. Cut into quarters and scoop out the seeds.

2 Finely chop the onion, chop the potato and slice the mushrooms.

3 Dry-fry the beef in a saucepan for 5 minutes, stirring until browned all over.

• Suitable for freezing.

Braised Beef and Carrots

Makes: 600ml/1 pint/2½ cups

175g/6oz potato
225g/8oz carrots
¼ onion
175g/6oz stewing beef
300ml/½ pint/1¼ cups water
pinch of dried mixed herbs

1 Preheat the oven to 180°C/ 350°F/Gas 4. Peel and chop the potato, carrots and onion and place in a flameproof casserole.

2 Rinse the beef, cut away any fat and gristle and cut into small cubes using a sharp knife.

3 Add the meat, water and herbs to the casserole, bring to the boil and then cover and cook in the oven for 1½ hours or until the meat is tender and the vegetables are soft.

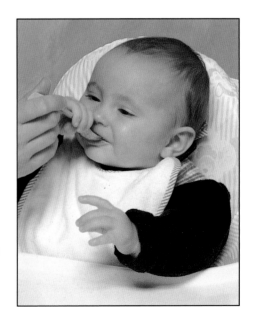

4 Process or mash the ingredients to the desired consistency and spoon a little into a bowl. Test the temperature and cool if necessary, before giving to baby.

5 Cover any unused food and transfer to the fridge as soon as possible. Use within 24 hours.

● Suitable for freezing.

TIP
Replace the carrots with any other root vegetable such as parsnip or swede, if wished.

Lamb Hotpot

Makes: 600ml/1 pint/2½ cups

| 115g/4oz potato |
| 115g/4oz carrot |
| 115g/4oz swede |
| 50g/2oz leek |
| 115g/4oz lamb fillet |
| 300ml/½ pint/1¼ cup water |
| pinch of dried rosemary |

1 Peel the potato, carrot and swede, rinse and chop into small cubes. Halve the leek lengthways, rinse well and slice. Place all the vegetables in a saucepan.

2 Rinse the lamb under cold water and chop into small pieces, discarding any fat.

3 Add the meat to the pan with the water and rosemary. Bring to the boil, cover and simmer for 30 minutes or until the lamb is thoroughly cooked.

4 Process or mash the ingredients to the desired consistency.

5 Spoon a little into a bowl, test the temperature and cool if necessary, before giving to baby.

6 Cover the remaining food and transfer to the fridge as soon as possible. Use within 24 hours.

- Suitable for freezing.

Lamb and Lentil Savoury

Makes: 600ml/1 pint/2½ cups

| 115g/4oz lamb fillet |
| 115g/4oz swede |
| 1 celery stick |
| 25g/1oz/2 tbsp red lentils |
| 15ml/1 tbsp tomato ketchup |
| 350ml/12fl oz/1½ cups water |

1 Rinse the lamb under cold water, trim off any fat and chop into small pieces. Peel the swede, place in a colander with the celery and rinse with cold water. Chop into cubes and place in a saucepan.

2 Put the lentils in a sieve and rinse under cold water, picking out any black bits. Add to the pan with the lamb and ketchup.

3 Add the water and bring to the boil, then cover and simmer for 40 minutes or until the lentils are soft. Top up with extra water during cooking if necessary, then process or mash just enough to give the desired consistency.

4 Spoon a little into a bowl, test the temperature and cool if necessary, before giving to baby.

5 Cover the remaining food and transfer to the fridge as soon as possible. Use within 24 hours.

● Suitable for freezing.

VARIATION
Substitute green lentils or split peas for the red lentils and a small courgette for the celery stick.

Country Pork and Green Beans

Makes: 450ml/¾ pint/1⅞ cups

115g/4oz lean pork
115g/4oz potato
115g/4oz carrot
75g/3oz runner beans
pinch of dried sage
350ml/12fl oz/1½ cups water

1 Rinse the pork under cold water, trim away any fat and gristle and chop into small cubes.

2 Peel the potato and carrot, trim the beans, rinse and chop.

3 Put the pork, potato and carrot in a saucepan with the sage and water. Bring to the boil, cover and simmer for 30 minutes.

4 Add the beans and cook, covered, for a further 10 minutes until all the vegetables are tender.

5 Process or mash to the desired consistency, then spoon a little into a bowl. Test the temperature before giving to baby.

6 Cover and transfer the remaining food to the fridge. Use within 24 hours.

- Suitable for freezing.

VARIATION

Instead of the pork, use any lean meat in this recipe, such as chicken or turkey. Add broad beans, with the outer skin removed, in place of the runner beans.

TIP
If runner beans are unavailable use French beans, sugar snap peas or broccoli. Look out for ready prepared diced pork in the supermarket. Cut into smaller pieces and make sure to remove any gristle before cooking.

Pork and Apple Savoury

Makes: 600ml/1 pint/2½ cups

175g/6oz lean pork
175g/6oz potato
175g/6oz swede or parsnip
¼ onion
½ dessert apple
300ml/½ pint/1¼ cups water
pinch of dried sage

1 Preheat the oven to 180°C/ 350°F/Gas 4. Rinse the pork under cold water, trim away any fat and gristle then chop. Peel and chop the vegetables. Peel, core and chop the apple.

2 Put the meat, vegetables, apple, water and sage in a flameproof casserole, cover and bring to the boil stirring once or twice.

3 Cover and cook in the oven for 1¼ hours until the meat is tender, then process or mash to the desired consistency.

4 Spoon a little into a bowl, test the temperature and cool if necessary, before giving to baby.

5 Cover the remaining food and transfer to the fridge as soon as possible. Use within 24 hours.

● Suitable for freezing.

TIP
The mixture can be cooked in a saucepan on the hob for 40 minutes if preferred.

Nursery Kedgeree

Makes: 600ml/1 pint/2½ cups

50g/2oz/¼ cup long grain rice

25g/1oz/2 tbsp frozen peas

350ml/12fl oz/1½ cups formula milk

90g/3¼oz brick frozen skinless cod

2 hard-boiled egg yolks

1 Place the rice, peas, milk and fish in a saucepan, bring to the boil, cover and simmer for 15 minutes, until the fish is cooked and the rice is soft.

2 Lift the fish out of the pan and break into pieces with a knife and fork, checking for bones.

3 Stir the fish into the rice mixture and add the egg yolks.

TIP
Peas can be quite difficult to mash down. Check before giving to baby as whole peas are difficult for baby to chew.

4 Mash with a fork to the desired consistency. Alternatively blend in a food processor, liquidizer or press through a sieve.

5 Spoon a little into a bowl, test the temperature and cool if necessary, before giving to baby.

6 Cover the remaining kedgeree and transfer to the fridge as soon as possible. Use within 24 hours.

● Suitable for freezing.

Mediterranean Vegetables

Makes: 600ml/1 pint/2½ cups

3 tomatoes
175g/6oz courgette
75g/3oz button mushrooms
115g/4oz red pepper
20ml/4 tsp tomato ketchup
250ml/8fl oz/1 cup water
pinch of dried mixed herbs
40g/1½oz dried pasta shapes

3 Rinse and slice the courgette and mushrooms. Chop the pepper.

4 Put the vegetables in a saucepan with the ketchup, water and herbs. Cover and simmer for 10 minutes or until tender.

5 Meanwhile cook the pasta in boiling water for 8–10 minutes until tender. Drain.

6 Mix the vegetables and pasta together and process or mash.

7 Spoon a little into a bowl, test the temperature and cool if necessary, before giving to baby.

8 Cover remaining mixture and refrigerate. Use within 24 hours.

● Suitable for freezing.

1 Make a cross cut in each tomato, put in a small bowl and cover with boiling water. Leave for 1 minute then drain and peel off the skins. Cut into quarters and scoop out the seeds from the tomatoes.

2 Trim the courgette and mushrooms and cut away the core and seeds from the pepper.

TIP
For adventurous eaters add ½ clove crushed garlic at Step 3.

Saucy Pasta

Makes: 600ml/1 pint/2½ cups

| 115g/4oz carrot |
| 50g/2oz Brussels sprouts |
| 25g/1oz green beans |
| 25g/1oz/2 tbsp frozen sweetcorn |
| 50g/2oz dried pasta shapes |
| 350ml/12fl oz/1½ cups formula milk |
| 50g/2oz mild Cheddar cheese |

1 Peel the carrot, discard any discoloured outer leaves from the sprouts and trim the beans. Rinse and then chop into pieces.

2 Place the vegetables, sweetcorn, pasta and milk in a saucepan, bring to the boil and then simmer, uncovered, for 12–15 minutes until the pasta is cooked.

TIP
Vary the vegetables depending on what you have in the fridge.

3 Grate the cheese and add to the vegetables, stirring until the cheese has completely melted.

4 Process or mash just enough to give the desired consistency, then spoon a little into a bowl. Test the temperature and cool if necessary, before giving to baby.

5 Cover the remaining food and transfer to the fridge as soon as possible. Use within 24 hours.

● Suitable for freezing.

Apple and Orange Fool

Makes: 250ml/8fl oz/1 cup

| 2 dessert apples |
| 5ml/1 tsp grated orange rind and 15ml/1 tbsp orange juice |
| 15ml/1 tbsp custard powder |
| 5ml/1 tsp caster sugar |
| 150ml/¼ pint/⅔ cup formula milk |

1 Quarter, core and peel the apples. Slice and place the apples in a saucepan with the orange rind and juice.

2 Cover and cook gently for 10 minutes, stirring occasionally until the apples are soft.

3 Blend the custard powder and sugar with a little of the milk to make a smooth paste. Bring the remaining milk to the boil and stir into the custard mixture.

4 Return the custard to the pan and slowly bring to the boil, stirring until thickened and smooth.

5 Process or mash the apple to the desired consistency. Add the custard and stir to mix.

6 Spoon a little into a bowl, test the temperature and cool if necessary, before giving to baby.

7 Cover the remaining fool and transfer to the fridge as soon as possible. Use within 24 hours.

• Suitable for freezing.

Orchard Fruit Dessert

Makes: 450ml/¾ pint/1⅞ cups

1 ripe pear
225g/8oz ripe plums
15ml/1 tbsp caster sugar
15ml/1 tbsp custard powder
150ml/¼ pint/⅔ cup formula milk

1 Quarter, core, peel and slice the pear. Wash the plums, then cut in half, stone and slice.

2 Put the fruit in a saucepan with 15ml/1 tbsp water and 10ml/2 tsp of the sugar. Cover and cook gently for 10 minutes until soft.

3 Blend the custard powder, remaining sugar and a little of the milk to a smooth paste.

4 Bring the remaining milk to the boil and gradually stir into the custard mixture. Pour the custard back into the pan and bring to the boil, stirring, until it is both thickened and smooth.

5 Process or mash the fruit to the desired consistency and stir in the custard. Spoon a little into a bowl, test the temperature and cool if necessary, before giving to baby.

6 Cover the remaining custard and transfer to the fridge as soon as possible. Use within 24 hours.

● Suitable for freezing.

Peach Melba Dessert

Makes: 175ml/6fl oz/¾ cup

1 ripe peach

25g/1oz fresh or frozen raspberries

15ml/1 tbsp icing sugar

115g/4oz natural Greek yogurt

1 Halve the peach, discard the stone then peel and slice. Place in a saucepan with the raspberries and 15ml/1 tbsp water.

2 Cover and cook gently for 10 minutes until soft.

3 Purée and press through a sieve to remove the raspberry pips.

TIP
The finished pudding is not suitable for freezing although the sweetened fruit purée can be frozen successfully in sections of an ice cube tray. Defrost cubes of purée and mix each cube with 15ml/ 1 tbsp yogurt.

4 Set aside to cool then stir in the sugar and swirl in the yogurt. Spoon a little into a baby dish.

5 Cover the remaining dessert and transfer to the fridge. Use within 24 hours.

VARIATION
Bananarama
To make a single portion, use ½ a small banana and 15ml/1 tbsp of natural Greek yogurt. Mash the banana until smooth and add the yogurt. Stir to mix and serve immediately. Do not make this dessert in advance, as the banana will discolour while standing.

STAGE 4: NINE TO TWELVE MONTHS

GRADUALLY PROGRESS FROM MINCED TO CHOPPED OR ROUGHLY MASHED FOOD. BY NOW YOUR BABY WILL BE ABLE TO JOIN IN WITH FAMILY MEALS AND EAT A LITTLE OF WHAT YOU ARE EATING. ENSURE THAT YOUR BABY IS EATING THREE MAIN MEALS AND TWO TO THREE SNACK MEALS PER DAY. YOUNG CHILDREN DEVELOP AT AN INCREDIBLY FAST RATE AND SO NEED TO EAT LITTLE AND OFTEN TO SUSTAIN ENERGY AND GROWTH LEVELS.

AGAIN FOODS FROM THE PREVIOUS SECTIONS CAN STILL BE SERVED TO YOUR BABY; JUST ADJUST THE TEXTURES AS NECESSARY.

Suitable Foods

FOODS TO INCLUDE
- whole eggs
- finely ground nuts
- more flavourings – stock cubes if part of a family-size casserole

- greater selection of finger foods – slices of peeled fruit (such as dessert apple or pear), raw carrot and cucumber sticks, small squares of cooked chicken

- selection of foods from the four main food groups

Apple, carrot and cucumber

Left: Finger foods – such as chopped raw vegetables and fruit pieces – come into their own at this age, and children love to help themselves.

Whole egg

Above: Inquisitive children love the time when they can join the family at the table.

Stock cubes

Ground nuts

FOODS TO AVOID
- keep salt to a minimum and omit if possible
- sugar: add just enough to make the food appetizing without being overly sweet
- honey
- fat: trim visible fat off raw meat, grill rather than fry
- organ meats – liver, kidney

Below: Though now a very small list, there are still some foods it is important to omit.

I can feed myself!

Encouraging your baby to feed herself can be a truly messy business. Some babies are interested from a very early age and those little fingers seem to move like lightning grabbing the bowl or the spoon you're using to feed them with. While foods are still finely puréed, give your baby a second spoon to play with, leaving you more able to spoon in the real lunch.

As your baby grows offer her a few finger foods to hold and hopefully eat, while you continue to feed from a spoon. Cooked carrot sticks, broccoli and cauliflower florets are soft on a young mouth and easy to chew. As your baby grows so you can introduce bread sticks and toast fingers.

Encourage your baby to pick up foods and as her co-ordination improves and she gets the idea, so more food will actually go where it is intended. Try to cut down on the mess by rolling up your baby's sleeves and covering clothes with a large bib, preferably with sleeves.

Above: *A bib with sleeves.*

Remove any hair bands and have a wet flannel at the ready.

Although it is tempting not to allow a baby feed herself, try not to be frustrated by the mess. Babies that are encouraged to feed themselves will probably be more adventurous later on and you will probably find there is less mess than

TEACHING YOUR BABY TO FEED ITSELF

1 Cover your baby well – this can be very messy! Give him a spoon of his own to play with.

2 While you are feeding your baby, allow him to play with the food – with his hands or the spoon.

3 Let your baby use the cup and spoon by himself. Don't worry about spillage – there are bound to be lots of slips at this stage.

4 Keep tissues or a damp flannel available and clean as you go. Be patient and take things slowly.

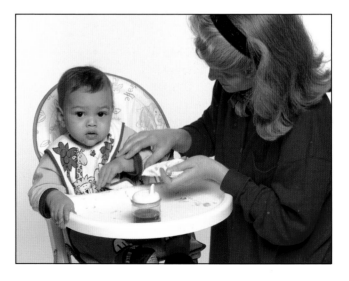

with a baby who is always spoon fed and keeps grabbing at the bowl. In addition, she will be able to join in your family meals and also give you the chance to eat your own meal before it goes cold.

WHAT TO DO IF YOUR CHILD CHOKES

● Don't waste time trying to remove food from your baby's mouth unless it can be done easily.
● Turn your baby, head down, supporting her head with your forearm and slap firmly between the shoulder blades.
● If this does not work, try again.
● Don't hesitate to ring your doctor or emergency services if worried.

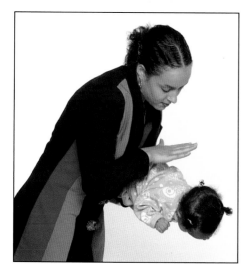

Above: *Don't be afraid to take quick, firm action in an emergency.*

COPING WITH THE MESS

As babies grow so too does the amount of mess! It can seem incredible how just a few tablespoons of lunch can be spread across so many surfaces and so many items of clothing.
● Choose a large bib. Fabric bibs with a plastic liner are the most comfortable for babies to wear when tiny, moving on to a plastic pelican-style bib to catch the bits as they grow older. Check the back of your

Above: *A hard plastic 'pelican' bib.*

baby's neck as these can rub.
● If you plan to feed your baby in the dining room, then protect the carpet with an old sheet, pieces of newspaper or plastic tablecloth or groundsheet. It is vital to take this with you if visiting friends.
● Give your baby a second spoon or small toy to play with so that she doesn't make a grab for the laden spoon.

Left: *It is a real delight when your baby can begin to feed independently. Not only can you start to eat with your baby, and relax a little more, but she will also enjoy setting her own pace and eating her meal in the order she chooses. At this stage the family can usually return to eating together around the table as a group.*

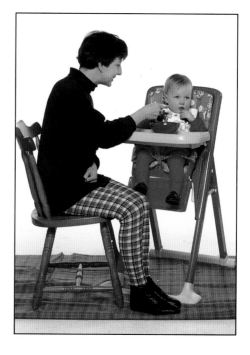

Above: *A plastic tablecloth or groundsheet on the floor will avoid carpet stains.*

FINGER FOODS

Finger foods are not only fun to eat but help your baby's co-ordination. Snacks play an important part in a young child's diet as appetites may be small, but energy and growth needs are great. Choose foods that are nutrient dense and avoid sweet sugary snacks such as chocolate biscuits.

Grapes

Plums

Celery

Carrots

Mini-sandwiches

Toast triangles

Chicken pieces

Fish fingers

Cheese cubes

Ham

Marmite fingers

Above: *Your baby can eat at her own pace until she is full.*

TIPS
● Always make sure baby is comfortable either on your lap or strapped into a baby chair or highchair.
● Check the temperature of the food and make sure it is not too hot.
● Change the texture of the food: some babies like quite wet mixtures, some hate lumps, some like a few lumps for interest, others prefer food they can pick up – tiny ham sandwiches, thick slices of grilled fishfinger, even picking up peas and sweetcorn.
● Encourage your baby to feed herself; don't worry about mess – your baby is still learning – but just mop up sticky hands and face at the end.
● Try to keep calm. If your baby keeps spitting food out, you may find it less upsetting to offer bought food rather than homemade so you don't feel you've been wasting your time cooking.
● Try not to let your baby see you're upset or cross. Even a one-year-old can sense the power she can have over you.
● If solid meals are well established, give her a drink at the end of the meal so that she is not full up with milk before she begins.
● Avoid biscuits and sweet things as your baby will soon learn that if she makes a fuss when the savoury is offered, then pudding will soon follow.
● Remember no baby will starve herself. Continue offering a variety of food and don't despair.

Above: *Give drinks at the end of the meal, or they will fill your baby up before he eats.*

Coping with a fussy eater

All children are fussy eaters at some stage. If mealtimes are always calm and plates always clean then your family must be one in a million. Even very young children learn the power they have over their parents and mealtimes give them a great opportunity to exercise it. Here are some common problems and advice on how to deal with them.

BABY SPITS OUT FOOD

You may be trying to wean your baby too soon or possibly she simply doesn't like the taste of the food. If you started with baby rice then go on to potato or parsnip purée or a little apple purée mixed into the baby rice. If that fails, your baby may simply not be ready for solids yet. Try again in a week or two's time.

BABY APPEARS TO GAG

Some babies just cannot cope with solids at first and may seem distressed and almost gag on the food. Try thinning down the food with a little more formula milk or water, since the food may be too thick. Alternatively, you may be putting too much food on the spoon; try offering the baby a little less. If neither of these seem to help, stop solids and breast or bottle feed as usual, giving her plenty of reassuring cuddles. Try again in a few days' or weeks' time. If your baby is nearly six months old then ask your health visitor or doctor for advice.

BABY SEEMS TO HAVE A SMALL APPETITE

Babies' appetites, like adults', vary enormously. Don't force feed your baby; if she's been eating well and then turns her head away or starts spitting it out, it's a pretty clear indication that she's had enough, even if the amount does seem very small to you. Resist the temptation to encourage the baby to clear the dish: it is never helpful to force children of any age, and can be extremely counterproductive. If you're worried, talk to your health visitor and regularly check your baby's weight.

Above: *Don't worry when you encounter resistance in feeding: there never has been a baby that likes all foods, all the time.*

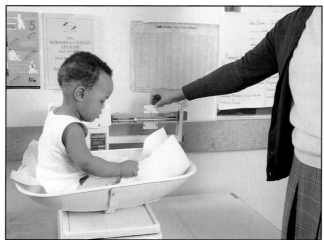

Left: *If you have serious anxieties, see your doctor or health visitor and get your baby's weight checked regularly.*

Going Vegetarian

A vegetarian diet can provide all the necessary nutrients for health and vitality, but it is important to balance the baby's diet to ensure that she receives adequate supplies of protein, vitamins D and B12, calcium and iron.

The basic guidelines are the same as for weaning any other baby; introduce flavours slowly and be guided by your baby. The biggest differences are obviously in the type of foods offered. Instead of obtaining protein from meat and fish, your baby will receive it from other protein-rich food. These include eggs, pulses, split lentils and grains, finely ground nuts or nut creams, sunflower seed spread, milk and dairy products and vegetarian cheese where available.

Vegetarians need to make sure that sufficient iron is included in their baby's diet. If she is over six months, offer prune juice, puréed apricots, molasses, refined lentils and cereals, particularly fortified breakfast cereals. Green vegetables and well-mashed beans, if over eight months, are also a good source of iron. Vitamin C aids absorption of iron from plant sources so make sure you serve fresh green vegetables or fruit in the meal. Your doctor may also feel it beneficial for your baby to take vitamin drops.

If you plan to bring the baby up as a vegan and so omit dairy products and eggs from the diet, then it is vital

to consult your doctor or dietician.

Vegetarian diets tend to be bulky and lower in calories than a diet containing meats so make sure you include foods which are protein and calorie rich, with little or no fibre, such as eggs, milk and cheese. These can be mixed with smaller quantities of vegetables, fruit and cereals. Fibre-rich foods can also be difficult

Above: *Raising your child as a vegetarian takes special planning and care.*

for a child to digest as many nutrients may pass straight through.

To ensure your baby is getting the correct amount of vitamins, minerals and food energy her diet should include foods from the four groups on the opposite page:

Oranges

Carrots

Cucumber

Grapes

Cereals and grains: rice around four months; pasta, bread, oats, and breakfast cereals from six months.

Fruit and vegetables: begin with potato, carrot, apple and pear around four months, progressing to stronger-flavoured foods as your baby develops.

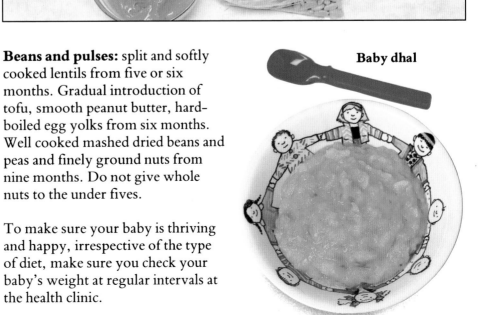

Dairy produce: including milk, cheese, fromage frais and yogurt from six months.
Note: Make sure cheese is rennet-free. If you are unsure, ask the delicatessen assistant, or check the packet if pre-packed.

Beans and pulses: split and softly cooked lentils from five or six months. Gradual introduction of tofu, smooth peanut butter, hard-boiled egg yolks from six months. Well cooked mashed dried beans and peas and finely ground nuts from nine months. Do not give whole nuts to the under fives.

To make sure your baby is thriving and happy, irrespective of the type of diet, make sure you check your baby's weight at regular intervals at the health clinic.

Baby dhal

Split peas

Lentils

The Importance of a Varied Diet

Once your baby progresses to more varied fruit and vegetable purées, you are really beginning to lay down the foundations for a healthy eating pattern and sound nutritional habits which will take your baby through childhood and into adult life.

It is vitally important to include portions of food from each of the four main food groups per day. But do make sure that the types of food you choose are suitable for the age of your child.

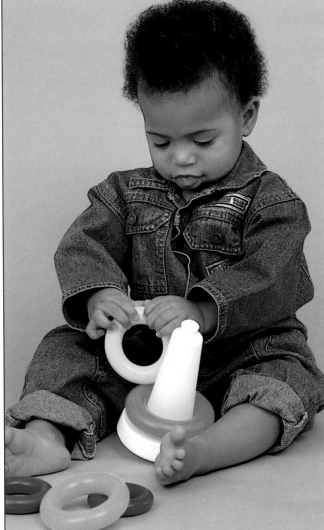

Left: *Your baby is now at the age where the diet can and should be as diverse as any adult's. Variety is crucial for health reasons, and also has the benefit of allowing you many options for tempting and maintaining the kind of interest in all types of food that will ensure good eating habits develop for the future.*

Group 1: *Cereals, bread, potatoes, rice and pasta*

Group 2: *Fruit and vegetables* – bland tastes to start, such as potato, swede and parsnip, then stronger flavours and a wider variety

Group 3: *Meat and meat alternatives* – meat, poultry, fish, eggs, pulses (peas, beans and lentils), tofu, finely ground nuts

Group 4: *Milk and milk products* – milk, including soya milk, cheese, yogurt (plain at first, then flavoured), fromage frais

There are two more food groups which add palatability to the diet as well as contributing energy.

Group 5: *Sugars*

Group 6: *Fats and oils*

It is not recommended you add sugar to baby foods or give lots of sugary drinks, particularly in the early days of weaning. Many of us have an inherent need for sweetness but to cater to this without building in bad habits try and include foods in the diet that are naturally sweet. Choose dessert apples instead of very sharp cooking apples, mix bananas or ripe apricots with sharper-tasting fruits.

For those foods that are very sharp try and add 5ml/1tsp sugar per portion, so they become palatable without being overly sweet. Given the choice your baby would prefer sweet flavours to savoury so make sure you include a good range of tastes in the diet. Too much sugar or

sweetened foods or drinks at this stage could lead to tooth decay before the teeth are even through.

Try to avoid offering biscuits as a mid-morning or afternoon snack. Try to encourage your baby to eat:

- a piece of banana
- a plain bread roll
- a few triangles of marmite toast
- a milky drink
- a small pot of fromage frais

Watch the amounts of fat and oil you include in the diet. Avoid frying especially when preparing first foods as young babies have difficulty digesting such foods. As your baby develops, you can spread toast fingers with a little butter or margarine or offer a few oven-baked chips as easy-to-hold finger foods. Maintain the milk feeds and introduce cows' milk (full-fat) after one year as the main drink of the day. Don't be tempted to serve skimmed milk as the valuable fat-soluble vitamins A and D will be lost, and your baby may not get the energy needed for growth.

HOMEMADE OR MANUFACTURED FOODS?

Most mothers use a combination of the two. Bought baby foods are convenient and often easier to use if going out for the day or until your baby's meals coincide with the rest

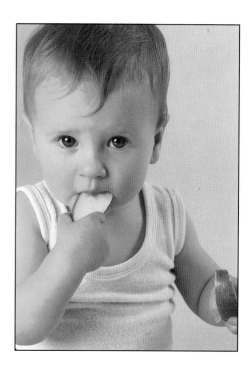

Above: *A piece of fruit or chopped vegetable is always preferable to a biscuit.*

of the family. Dried baby foods can be useful in the very early days when baby is eating only a teaspoon of food at each meal. On the other hand, homemade foods can be batch cooked or made with some of the ingredients from the main family meal and are often less trouble than you would expect. Added to this is the satisfaction of knowing your baby has eaten a wholesome meal and hopefully is acquiring a taste for home cooking.

Left: *Don't always assume that all homemade foods are better and more nutritional than all manufactured foods. There are now some excellent products available for purchase which can save you time and effort and add hugely to your repertoire without any loss of dietary values.*

Lamb Couscous

Makes: 750ml/1⅓ pint/3⅓ cups

115g/4oz carrot
115g/4oz swede
¼ onion
175g/6oz lamb fillet
5ml/1 tsp oil
10ml/2 tsp vegetable purée
30ml/2 tbsp currants
300ml/½ pint/1¼ cups water
50g/2oz couscous

1 Peel the carrot, swede and onion, rinse and chop. Rinse the lamb, trim off any fat, and chop.

2 Heat the oil in a saucepan, and fry the lamb until browned.

3 Add the vegetables, cook for 2 minutes then stir in the vegetable purée, currants and water. Cover and simmer for 25 minutes.

4 Rinse the couscous in a sieve. Cover and steam the couscous over the lamb pan, for 5 minutes.

5 Chop or process the lamb mixture to the desired consistency. Fluff up the couscous with a fork and add to the lamb mixture stirring well.

6 Spoon a little into a bowl, test the temperature and cool if necessary, before giving to baby.

7 Cover the remaining food and transfer to the fridge as soon as possible. Use within 24 hours.

● Suitable for freezing.

TIP
Look out for vegetable purée in tubes on the same shelf as the tomato purée in the supermarket.

Paprika Pork

Makes: 600ml/1 pint/2½ cups

175g/6oz lean pork
75g/3oz carrot
175g/6oz potato
¼ onion
¼ red pepper
5ml/1tsp oil
2.5ml/½ tsp paprika
150g/5oz/⅔ cup baked beans
150ml/¼ pint/⅔ cup water

1 Preheat the oven to 180°C/ 350°F/Gas 4. Rinse the pork under cold water, pat dry and trim away any fat or gristle. Cut the pork into small cubes.

2 Peel the carrot, potato and onion. Cut away the core and remove any seeds from the pepper. Put into a colander, rinse under cold water then chop into small pieces.

TIP
If using a food processor to chop baby dinner, drain off most of the liquid. Process then stir in liquid until desired texture is reached.

3 Heat the oil in a flameproof casserole, add the pork and fry for a few minutes, stirring until browned. Add the vegetables, cook for 2 minutes then add the paprika, baked beans and water.

4 Bring back to the boil, then cover and cook in the oven for 1¼ hours until the pork is tender.

5 Chop or process the casserole to the desired consistency, then spoon a little into a bowl. Test the temperature and cool if necessary, before giving to baby.

6 Cover the remaining food and transfer to the fridge as soon as possible. Use within 24 hours.

• Suitable for freezing.

Chicken and Celery Supper

Makes: 600ml/1 pint/2½ cups

175g/6oz chicken thighs, skinned and boned
¼ onion
225g/8oz carrots
75g/3oz celery
5ml/1 tsp oil
10ml/2 tsp vegetable purée
250ml/8fl oz/1 cup water

1 Rinse the chicken under cold water, pat dry, trim off any fat and cut into chunks.

2 Trim and rinse the vegetables and cut into small pieces.

3 Heat the oil in a saucepan, add the chicken and onion and fry for a few minutes, stirring until browned. Add the carrots, celery, vegetable purée and water. Bring to the boil, cover and simmer for 20 minutes until tender.

4 Chop or process the mixture to the desired consistency. If using a food processor, process the solids first and then add the liquid a little at a time.

5 Spoon a little into a bowl, test the temperature and cool if necessary, before giving to baby.

6 Cover the remaining casserole and transfer to the fridge as soon as possible. Use within 24 hours.

• Suitable for freezing.

TIP
For extra flavour, add homemade stock instead of the water, or use commercial stock, but make sure it does not have a high sodium level.

Cauliflower and Broccoli Cheese

Makes: 600ml/1 pint/2½ cups

175g/6oz cauliflower

175g/6oz broccoli

175g/6oz potato

300ml/½ pint/1¼ cups formula milk

75g/3oz mild Cheddar cheese

1 Rinse the vegetables, then break the cauliflower and broccoli into florets. Slice the tender stems but cut out and discard any woody core from the cauliflower. Peel and chop the potatoes into cubes.

2 Place the vegetables and milk in a saucepan, bring to the boil, cover and simmer for 12–15 minutes until quite tender.

3 Grate the cheese and add to the vegetables stirring until the cheese has melted.

4 Process or mash the mixture to the desired consistency, adding a little extra milk if necessary.

5 Spoon a little into a bowl, test the temperature and cool if necessary, before serving to baby.

6 Cover the remaining food and transfer to the fridge as soon as possible. Use within 24 hours.

● Suitable for freezing.

Cheesy Tagliatelle with Broccoli and Ham

Makes: 600ml/1 pint/2½ cups

115g/4oz broccoli

50g/2oz wafer thin ham

50g/2oz Cheddar cheese

300ml/½ pint/1¼ cups formula milk

50g/2oz tagliatelle

1 Rinse the broccoli and cut into small florets, chopping the stalks. Chop the ham and grate the Cheddar cheese.

2 Pour the formula milk into a saucepan, bring to the boil and add the tagliatelle. Simmer uncovered for 5 minutes.

3 Add the broccoli and cook for 10 minutes until tender.

TIP
Pasta swells on standing so you may need to thin the cooled leftover mixture with extra formula milk before reheating.

4 Add the ham and cheese to the broccoli and pasta, stirring until the cheese has melted.

5 Chop or process the mixture to the desired consistency and then spoon a little into a bowl. Test the temperature and cool if necessary, before giving to baby.

6 Cover the remaining food and transfer to the fridge as soon as possible. Use within 24 hours.

• Suitable for freezing.

Baby Dahl

Makes: 600ml/1 pint/2½ cups

50g/2oz/¼ cup red lentils
¼ onion
2.5ml/½ tsp ground coriander
1.25ml/¼ tsp turmeric
350ml/12fl oz/1½ cups water
75g/3oz potato
75g/3oz carrot
75g/3oz cauliflower
75g/3oz green cabbage

1 Rinse the lentils under cold water, discarding any black bits.

2 Chop onion, add to saucepan with lentils, spices and water.

3 Bring to the boil, cover and simmer for 20 minutes.

4 Chop the potato, carrot and cabbage. Break the cauliflower into small florets.

5 Stir the vegetables into the pan. Cook for 12–15 minutes.

6 Chop or process the dahl to the desired consistency, adding a little extra boiled water if necessary.

7 Spoon a little dahl into a bowl, test the temperature and cool if necessary, before serving to baby.

8 Cover the remaining dahl and transfer to the fridge as soon as possible. Use within 24 hours.

• Suitable for freezing.

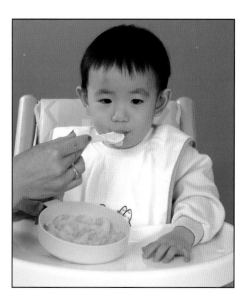

Cheesy Fish Pie

Makes: 450ml/¾ pint/1⅞ cups

| 225g/8oz potato |
| 50g/2oz leek |
| 50g/2oz button mushrooms |
| 90g/3½oz brick frozen skinless cod |
| 250ml/8fl oz/1 cup formula milk |
| 50g/2oz Cheddar cheese, grated |

1 Peel the potato, halve the leek and trim the mushrooms. Place all the vegetables in a colander and rinse well with cold water, drain, then chop the vegetables.

2 Place the vegetables in a saucepan with the frozen fish and milk. Bring to the boil, cover and simmer for 15 minutes, until the fish is cooked and the potatoes are tender when pierced with a knife.

3 Lift the fish out of pan with a slotted spoon and break into pieces with a knife and fork checking carefully for bones.

4 Return the fish to the pan and stir in the grated cheese. Chop or process the mixture to give the desired consistency.

5 Spoon a little into a bowl, test the temperature and cool if necessary, before serving to baby.

6 Cover the remaining fish pie and transfer to the fridge as soon as possible. Use within 24 hours.

● Suitable for freezing.

Fish Creole

Makes: 450ml/¾ pint/1⅞ cups

50g/2oz celery

50g/2oz red pepper

300ml/½ pint/1¼ cups water

50g/2oz/¼ cup long grain rice

10ml/2 tsp tomato ketchup

90g/3¼oz brick frozen skinless cod

1 Trim the celery and discard the core and seeds from the pepper. Rinse and chop the vegetables.

2 Bring the water to the boil in a saucepan and add the vegetables, rice, ketchup and fish.

3 Bring back to the boil, then reduce heat, cover and simmer for 15 minutes, until the rice is tender and the fish is cooked.

4 Lift the fish out of the pan with a slotted spoon. Use a knife and fork to check for bones.

6 Spoon a little fish mixture into a small bowl, test the temperature and cool if necessary, before giving to baby.

7 Cover the leftover fish creole and transfer to the fridge as soon as possible. Use within 24 hours.

● Suitable for freezing.

5 Stir the fish back into the pan and then chop or process.

Chocolate Pots

Makes: 2

5ml/1 tsp cocoa
5ml/1 tsp caster sugar
150ml/¼ pint/⅔ cup formula or cows' milk
1 egg

1 Preheat the oven to 180°C/ 350°F/Gas 4. Blend the cocoa and sugar with a little of the milk in a small bowl to make a smooth paste. Stir in the remaining milk and then pour the mixture into a saucepan.

2 Bring just to the boil. Beat the egg in a bowl then gradually stir in the hot milk, mixing well until the mixture is smooth.

3 Strain the mixture into two ramekin dishes to remove any egg solids.

4 Place the dishes in a roasting tin or shallow cake tin. Pour boiling water into the tin to come halfway up the sides of the dishes.

5 Cook in the oven for 15–20 minutes or until the custard has set. Leave to cool.

6 Transfer to the fridge as soon as possible. Serve one pudding and use the second within 24 hours.

Vanilla Custards

Makes: 2

1 egg

5ml/1 tsp caster sugar

few drops vanilla essence

150ml/¼ pint/⅔ cup formula or
  cows' milk

1 Preheat the oven to 180°C/
350°F/Gas 4. Using a fork, beat
the egg, sugar and vanilla essence
together in a bowl.

2 Pour the milk into a small
saucepan and heat until it is just
to the boil.

3 Gradually stir the milk into the
egg mixture, whisking or
beating until smooth.

4 Strain into two ramekin dishes
and place in a roasting tin. Add
enough boiling water to come
halfway up the sides of the dishes.

5 Bake for 15–20 minutes or until
the custard has set. Cool and
serve as for **Chocolate Pots**.

Marmite Bread Sticks

Makes: 36

little oil, for greasing

150g/5oz packet pizza base mix

flour, for dusting

5ml/1 tsp Marmite

1 egg yolk

1 Brush two baking sheets with a little oil. Put the pizza mix in a bowl, add the quantity of water as directed on the packet and mix to make a smooth dough.

2 Knead on a lightly floured surface for 5 minutes until smooth and elastic.

3 Roll out to a 23cm/9in square. Cut into strips 7.5cm × 1cm/3 × ½in, twisting each to give a corkscrew effect. Arrange on the baking sheets, slightly spaced apart.

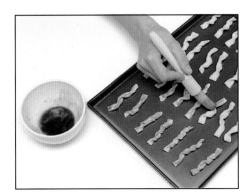

4 Mix the Marmite and egg yolk together and brush over the bread sticks. Loosely cover with oiled clear film and leave in a warm place for 20–30 minutes to rise.

5 Meanwhile preheat the oven to 220°C/425°F/Gas 7. Bake the bread sticks for 8–10 minutes until well risen. Loosen but leave to cool on the baking sheet.

6 Serve one or two sticks to baby. Store the rest in a plastic box for up to three days.

• Suitable for freezing up to three months in a plastic bag.

Eggy Bread Fingers

Makes: 16

2 slices bread

1 egg

30ml/2 tbsp formula or cows' milk

little butter and oil, for frying

1 Trim the crusts off the bread, then cut each slice in half.

2 Beat the egg and milk in a shallow dish and dip the bread, one slice at a time, into the egg until coated on both sides.

3 Heat a little butter and oil in a frying pan. Add the bread and fry until browned on both sides.

4 Cool slightly, cut into fingers and serve to baby as finger food or as part of a meal.

Cheese Straws

Makes: 42

little oil for greasing

175g/6oz/1½ cups plain flour

75g/3oz/6 tbsp butter or margarine,
 cut into pieces

115g/4oz Cheddar cheese, grated

1 egg, beaten

1 Preheat the oven to 200°C/
 400°F/Gas 6. Brush two baking
sheets lightly with oil.

2 Place the flour in a bowl, add the
 butter or margarine and rub in
until the mixture resembles fine
breadcrumbs. Stir in the grated
Cheddar cheese.

3 Reserve 15ml/1 tbsp beaten egg
 and then stir the rest into the
pastry mixture. Mix to a smooth
dough, adding water if necessary.

4 Knead lightly and roll out on a
 floured surface to a rectangle
30 × 20cm/12 × 8in. Brush with
remaining egg.

5 Cut into strips 7.5 × 1cm/
 3 × ½in and place on the baking
sheets, spaced slightly apart.

6 Bake in the oven for 8–10
 minutes until golden brown.
Loosen from but leave to cool on the
baking sheets.

7 Serve one or two sticks to baby
 and store the rest in a plastic box
for up to 1 week.

● Suitable for freezing up to three
months in a plastic box, interleaved
with greaseproof paper.

TIP
Begin making these with mild
cheese and as your child gets more
adventurous change to stronger
flavoured cheese.

Mini Cup Cakes

Makes: 26

50g/2oz/4 tbsp soft margarine

50g/2oz/¼ cup caster sugar

50g/2oz/⅓ cup self-raising flour

1 egg

1 Preheat the oven to 180°C/ 350°F/Gas 4. Separate 26 paper mini muffin cases and place on a large baking sheet.

2 Put all the ingredients for the cake into a mixing bowl and beat together well until smooth.

3 Divide the mixture among the cases and cook for 8–10 minutes until well risen and golden.

4 Transfer cakes to a wire rack and leave to cool completely, then peel the paper off one or two cakes and serve to baby.

5 Store the remaining cakes in a plastic box for up to three days.

● Suitable for freezing up to three months in a plastic box.

TIP
Cut a cup cake in half crossways and spread one half with a little sugar-free jam. Replace top half and serve to baby.

Shortbread Shapes

Makes: 60

little oil, for greasing
150g/5oz/1 cup plain flour
25g/1oz/3 tbsp cornflour
50g/2oz/¼ cup caster sugar
115g/4oz/½ cup butter
extra sugar, for sprinkling (optional)

1 Preheat the oven to 180°C/ 350°F/Gas 4. Brush two baking sheets with a little oil.

2 Put the flour, cornflour and sugar in a bowl. Cut the butter into pieces and rub into the flour until the mixture resembles fine breadcrumbs. Mould to a dough with your hands.

3 Knead lightly and roll out on a floured surface to a 5mm/¼in thickness. Stamp out shapes with small biscuit or petits fours cutters.

4 Transfer to the baking sheets, sprinkle with extra sugar, if liked, and cook for 10–12 minutes until pale golden. Loosen with a knife and leave to cool on the baking sheets, then transfer to a wire rack.

5 Offer baby one or two shapes and store the rest in a plastic box for up to one week.

TIP
These biscuits will keep well in the freezer for three months. Pack in rigid plastic boxes and thaw in a single layer. If you prefer, you can freeze the biscuits before baking. Wrap well to prevent them taking up flavours from other food.

FOOD FOR TODDLERS

Once your child has reached 12 months he or she will be enjoying a varied diet and eating habits and their personal food preferences will be developing. It is now vitally important to lay the foundations of a good and well balanced eating regime.

This is a time when food fads may also develop. Try to weather this period of fussy eating – all children will experience it at some time, and even good eaters will go through a picky stage. Hopefully the fad will go as quickly as it comes, but while it lasts mealtimes can become a nightmare.

Coping With a Fussy Eater

We all have different sized appetites whatever our age, and young children are no exception. Children's appetites fluctuate greatly and often tail off just before a growth spurt. All children go through food fads; some just seem to last longer and be more difficult than others.

A toddler's appetite varies enormously and you may find that she will eat very well one day and eat hardly anything the next. Be guided by your toddler and try to think in terms of what the child has eaten over several days rather than just concentrating on one day.

At the time, it can be really frustrating and worrying. Try not to think of the food that you have just thrown away but try to think more in the long term. Jot down the foods that your child has actually eaten over three or four days or up to a week. You may actually be surprised, it's not just yogurts and crisps after all!

Once you have a list you may find a link between the foods your child eats and the time of day. Perhaps your child eats better when eating with the family, or when the house is quiet. If you do find a link then build on it. You might find that your child is snacking on chocolate, doughnuts, soft drinks or chips when out with friends, and that fussiness at home is really a full tummy. Or it may be that by cutting out a milky drink and a biscuit mid-morning and offering a sliced apple instead, your child may not be so full up come lunch time. Perhaps you could hide the biscuit tin once visitors have had one, so that tiny hands can't keep reaching for more.

If your toddler seems hungrier at breakfast then you could offer eggy bread, a grilled sausage or a few banana slices with her cereal.

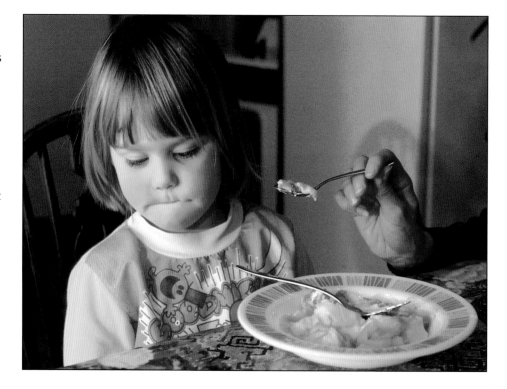

Above: *Don't panic about food rejection. Be patient and keep a journal listing what your child actually does eat.*

Right: *Fresh, healthy snacks will preserve the appetite for main meals.*

Although this all sounds obvious, when rushing about caring for a toddler and perhaps an older child or new baby, life becomes rather blurred and it can be difficult to stand back and look at things objectively.

REFUSING TO EAT

A child will always eat if she is hungry although it may not be when you want her to eat. A child can stay fit and healthy on surprisingly little. Providing your child is growing and gaining weight then don't fuss, but if you are worried, talk to your health visitor or doctor. Take the lead from your child, never force feed a child and try not to let meal times become a battle ground.

MAKING MEAL TIMES FUN

Coping with a fussy eater can be incredibly frustrating. The less she eats the crosser you get and so the spiral goes on as your toddler learns how to control meal times. To break this vicious circle, try diffusing things by involving your child in the preparation of the meal. You could pack up a picnic with your child's help, choosing together what to take. Then go somewhere different to eat, it could be the back garden, the swings or even the car. Alternatively, have a dollies' or teddies' tea party or make a camp under the dining table or even in the cupboard under the stairs.

Even very young children enjoy having friends for tea. If your child is going through a fussy or non-eating stage, invite over a little friend with a good appetite. Try to take a back seat and don't make a fuss over how much the visiting child eats.

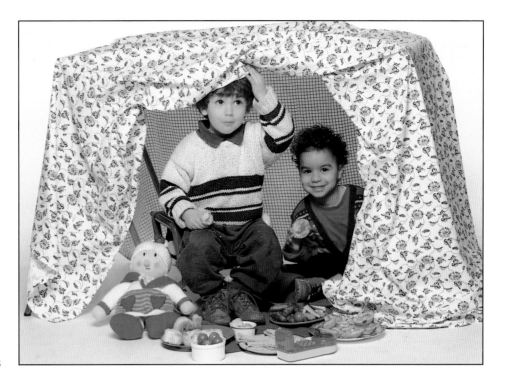

Above: *Changing the scene and breaking routine can help a lot.*

Below: *Making the meal a special event can distract the child from any eating worries.*

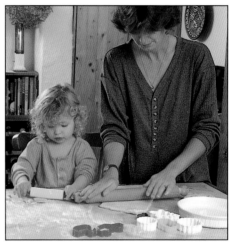

Above: *Getting your child to help you cook the food will encourage them to eat it, too.*

Above: *Children are more likely to eat with friends of their own age around them.*

10 TIPS TO COPE WITH A FUSSY EATER

1 Try to find meals that the rest of the family enjoys and where there are at least one or two things the fussy child will eat as well. It may seem easier to cook only foods that your child will eat but it means a very limited diet for everyone else and your child will never get the chance to have a change of mind and try something new.

2 Serve smaller portions of food to your child.

3 Invite round her friend with a hearty appetite. A good example sometimes works but don't comment on how much the visiting child has eaten.

4 Invite an adult who the child likes for supper – a granny, uncle or friend. Sometimes a child will eat for someone else without any fuss at all.

5 Never force feed a child.

6 If your child is just playing with the food and won't eat, quietly remove the plate without fuss and don't offer pudding.

7 Try to make meal times enjoyable and talk about what the family has been doing.

8 Try limiting snacks and drinks between meals so your child feels hungrier when it comes to family meal times. Alternatively, offer more nutritious snacks and smaller main meals if your child eats better that way.

9 Offer drinks after a meal so that they don't spoil the appetite.

10 Offer new foods when you know your child is hungry and hopefully more receptive.

Above: *Remember to give drinks after the meal, not before.*

EATING TOGETHER

Eating together as a family should be a happy part of the day, but can turn into a nightmare if everyone is tired or you feel as though the only things your children will eat are chips.

There is nothing worse than preparing a lovely supper, laying the table and sitting down with everyone and then one child refuses to eat, shrieks her disapproval or just pushes the food around the plate. However hard you try to ignore this behaviour, the meal is spoilt for everyone, especially if this is a regular occurrence. It's not fair on you or anyone else.

If you feel this is just a passing phase, then you could try just ignoring it and carry on regardless. Try to praise the good things, perhaps the way the child sits nicely at the table or the way she holds a knife and fork. Talk about the things that have been happening in the day, rather than concentrating on the meal itself. Try to avoid comparing your child's appetite with more hearty eaters. With luck, this particular fad will go away.

However, if it becomes a regular thing and mealtimes always seem more like a battleground than a happy family gathering, perhaps it's time for a sterner approach.

First steps

● Check to see if there is something physically wrong with your child. Has she been ill? If she has, she may not have recovered fully. If you're worried, then ask your doctor.
● Perhaps your child has enlarged adenoids or tonsils which could make swallowing difficult, or perhaps she has a food allergy, such as coeliacs disease – an intolerance to gluten – which may be undiagnosed but which would give the child tummy pains after eating. Again, check with your doctor.
● Is your child worried or stressed? If your family circumstances have changed – a new baby perhaps, or if you've moved recently – your child may be unhappy or confused.
● Is your child trying to get your attention?

Above: *Good seating of the right height will contribute to comfort and relaxation.*

Secondly

Look at the way in which you as a family eat. Do you eat at regular times? Do you sit down to eat or catch snacks on the move? Do you enjoy your food or do you always feel rushed and harassed? Children will pick up habits from their parents – bad as well as good. If you don't tend to sit down to a meal or you have the habit of getting up during meal times to do other jobs, then it's hard to expect the child to behave differently.

Finally

Talk things over with all the family. If you all feel enough is enough, then it's time to make a plan of action. Explain that from now on you are all going to eat together where possible, when and where you say so. You will choose the food, there will be three meals a day and no snacks. Since milk is filling and dulls the appetite, milky drinks will only be given after a meal; during the meal water or juice will be provided.

It is vitally important to involve all the family in this strategy so that there is no dipping into the biscuit tin or raiding the cupboard for crisps after school. Make sure that the fussy eater is aware of what is going to happen and give a few days' notice so that the idea can sink in.

Once you have outlined your strategy, work out your menus and

stick to them. Include foods your child definitely likes, chicken or carrots for instance, and obviously avoid foods your child hates although you could introduce some new foods for variety. Set yourself a time scale, perhaps one or two weeks, and review things after this period has elapsed.

PUTTING THE PLAN INTO ACTION

Begin your new plan of action when all the family are there to help, such as a weekend, and stick to it. Make a fuss of the plans so it seems more like a game than a prison sentence. Add a few flowers to the table or a pretty cloth to make it more special.

Begin the day with a normal breakfast but give the fussy eater the smallest possible portion. If the child eats it up then offer something you know your child likes, such as an apple, a few raisins or a fruit yogurt.

As the days progress, you could offer a biscuit or milkshake as a treat.

Give plenty of encouragement and praise, but be firm if the child plays up. If she behaves badly, take her to a different room or to the bottom of the stairs and explain that the only food is that on the table. Sit down with the rest of the family, leaving the fussy eater's food on the table and try to ignore the child.

If the child changes her mind just as you're about to clear away, then get the other members of the family to come back to the table and wait until the fussy eater has finished.

Continue in this way with other meals. Don't be swayed if your child says she will eat her food watching TV or if she wants her pudding first. Explain that she must eat just like everyone else or go without.

If she begins to cry, sit her down in another room and return to the table. This is perhaps the hardest thing of all.

After a few days, there should be a glimmer of progress. Still offer tiny portions of food, followed by foods that you know your child will eat as a treat. Keeping to a plan like this is hard, but if all the family sticks together and thinks positively, then it is possible. Keep to the time span you decided, then suggest you all go to your local pizza or burger restaurant and let the fussy eater choose what she likes.

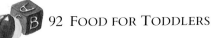

A Balanced and Varied Diet

Give your child a selection of foods in the four main food groups daily:

Cereal and filler foods: include three to four helpings of the following per day – breakfast cereals, bread, pasta, potatoes, rice.

Fruit and vegetables: try to have three or four helpings per day. Choose from fresh, canned, frozen or dried.

Meat and/or alternatives: one to two portions per day – meat – all kinds, including burgers and sausages, poultry, fish (fresh, canned or frozen), eggs (well-cooked), lentils and pulses (for example baked beans, red kidney beans, chick-peas), finely chopped nuts, smooth peanut butter, seeds, tofu, and Quorn.

Dairy foods: include 1 pint of milk per day or a mix of milk, cheese, yogurt and fromage frais. For a child who goes off drinking milk, try flavouring it or using it in custards, ice cream, rice pudding or cheese sauce. A carton of yogurt or 40g/1½oz of cheese have the same amount of calcium as 190ml/⅓ pint of milk.

THE IMPORTANCE OF BREAKFAST

Breakfast is a vitally important start for any young child. Count back: your child may have had tea at 5 o'clock the previous day and if she misses breakfast at 8 o'clock she will not have eaten for 15 hours. Allow time to sit down and don't hurry your child. Offer milk and cereals, orange juice diluted with a little water (not squash), a few slices of fruit and half a piece of toast preferably spread with smooth peanut butter or Marmite.

Above: *Cereal and filler foods, like bread, pasta and rice.*

Above: *Fruit and vegetables, including frozen, dried and canned goods.*

Above: *Meat and meat alternatives, like pulses and nuts.*

Above: *Dairy foods such as milk, cheese and yogurt.*

Marmite toast

Sliced pears

FATS

As adults we are all aware of the need to cut down on our fat consumption, but when eating together as a family, bear in mind that fat is a useful source of energy in a child's diet. The energy from fat is in concentrated form, so that your child can take in the calories she needs for growth and development before her stomach becomes overfull. Fat in food is also a valuable source of the fat-soluble vitamins, A, D, E and K, as well as essential fatty acids that the body cannot make by itself.

In general, fat is best provided by foods which contain not just fat but other essential nutrients as well, such as dairy products, eggs, meat and fish. Whole milk and its products such as cheese and yogurt, and eggs contain the fat-soluble vitamins A and D, while sunflower oil, nuts and oily fish are a good source of various essential fatty acids.

It is wise to cut down on deep frying and to grill or oven bake foods where possible. All children love chips and crisps but do keep them as a treat rather than a daily snack.

FRUIT AND VEGETABLES

Fresh fruit and vegetables play an essential part in a balanced diet. Offer fresh fruit, such as slices of apple or banana, for breakfast and tea, and perhaps thin sticks of raw carrot and celery for lunch. Instead of biscuits and crisps, offer your child raisins, ready-to-eat apricots, satsumas or carrots and apple slices if she wants a mid-morning or afternoon snack. Keep the fruit bowl within easy reach so your child may be tempted to pick up a banana as she walks through the kitchen.

Above: *A good mixture of the four basic food types will provide maximum energy and vitality for growing children.*

SNACKS

Young children cannot eat enough food at mealtimes to meet their needs for energy and growth and snacks can play a vital part in meeting these needs. However keep chocolate biscuits and crisps as a treat. They contain little goodness and are bad for the teeth. At meal times keep sweets out of sight until the main course has been eaten.

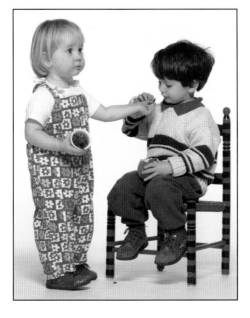

Above: *Do keep sweets and chocolate as treats – give fruit and vegetables as day-to-day snacks.*

Bread sticks

Courgettes

Melon

Broccoli

Sultanas

Raisins

Dried apricots

LUNCH SPECIALS

NOW YOUR BABY HAS PROGRESSED FROM PURÉED TO CHOPPED FOOD YOU CAN BEGIN TO COOK MORE GROWN-UP LUNCHES. TRY TO INTRODUCE A RANGE OF FOODS TO GIVE A BALANCED DIET AND A VARIETY OF TASTES ALTHOUGH DON'T BE DISHEARTENED IF THERE ARE A FEW HICCUPS ALONG THE WAY.

Sticky Chicken

Serves 2–4

4 chicken drumsticks

10ml/2 tsp oil

5ml/1 tsp soy sauce

15ml/1 tbsp smooth peanut butter

15ml/1 tbsp tomato ketchup

small jacket potatoes, sweetcorn and tomato wedges, to serve

1 Preheat the oven to 200°C/ 400°F/Gas 6 and line a small shallow baking tin with foil. Rinse the drumsticks under cold water, pat dry and peel off the skin. Make three or four slashes in the meat with a sharp knife and place in the tin.

2 Blend the remaining ingredients and spread thickly over the top of the chicken drumsticks. Cook in the oven for 15 minutes.

3 Turn the drumsticks over and baste with the peanut butter mixture and meat juices.

TIP
If more convenient, use the peanut butter and ketchup mixture over chicken thighs or kebabs instead.

4 Cook for a further 20 minutes or until the juices run clear when the chicken is pierced with a knife.

5 Cool slightly, then wrap a small piece of foil around the base of each drumstick. Arrange on plates and serve with small jacket potatoes, hot sweetcorn and tomato wedges.

Coriander Chicken Casserole

Serves 2

2 chicken thighs

¼ small onion

1 small carrot, about 50g/2oz

1 small piece swede, about 50g/2oz

5ml/1 tsp oil

2.5ml/½ tsp ground coriander

pinch of turmeric

5ml/1 tsp plain flour

150ml/¼ pint/⅔ cup chicken stock

salt and pepper (optional)

mashed potatoes and peas, to serve

1 Preheat the oven to 180°C/ 350°F/Gas 4. Rinse the chicken under cold water, pat dry and trim away any excess skin if necessary. Chop the onion, carrot and swede.

2 Heat the oil in a frying pan, add the chicken and brown on each side. Add the vegetables.

TIP
Chop the meat for very young toddlers. Serve older children the whole thigh to make them feel more grown up, then help with cutting.

3 Stir in the coriander, turmeric and flour, then add the stock and a little salt and pepper, if liked. Bring to the boil then transfer to a casserole.

4 Cover and cook in the oven for 1 hour. Spoon onto serving plates or into shallow dishes, cool slightly and serve the chicken casserole with mashed potatoes and peas.

Cheesy Chicken Parcels

Serves 2

1 boned and skinned chicken breast, about 150g/5oz

25g/1oz Cheddar cheese

1 slice lean ham, cut into 4 strips

15ml/1 tbsp oil

new potatoes, broccoli and carrots, to serve

1 Rinse the chicken under cold water, pat dry and cut in half crossways. Place each half between two pieces of clear film and flatten slightly with a rolling pin until each piece is about 10cm/4in square.

2 Cut the cheese in half and place a piece on each escalope. Wrap the chicken around the cheese to enclose it completely.

3 Arrange two pieces of the ham crossways over each of the parcels, securing them underneath with cocktail sticks. Brush the chicken parcels with oil.

TIP
You could wrap the parcels with halved rashers of rindless streaky bacon, if preferred.

4 Place on a piece of foil and chill until ready to cook.

5 Preheat the grill. Cook the chicken for 10 minutes, turning once, until browned. Remove the cocktail sticks, cool slightly, then arrange on two plates and serve with new potatoes, steamed broccoli florets and sliced carrots.

Peppered Beef Casserole

Serves 2

115g/4oz lean braising steak

¼ small onion

¼ small red pepper

¼ small yellow pepper

5ml/1 tsp oil

30ml/2 tbsp canned red kidney beans, drained and rinsed

5ml/1 tsp plain flour

150ml/¼ pint/⅔ cup lamb stock

15ml/1 tbsp tomato ketchup

5ml/1 tsp Worcestershire sauce

45ml/3 tbsp couscous

a few drops of oil

40g/1½oz/3 tbsp frozen peas

salt and pepper (optional)

4 Bring to the boil, stirring, then transfer to a casserole dish, cover and cook in the oven for about 1½ hours, or until the meat is tender.

5 Just before serving place the couscous in a bowl, cover with boiling water and leave to soak for 5 minutes. Drain into a sieve and stir in a few drops of oil.

6 Bring a saucepan of water to the boil, add the peas, and place the sieve of couscous over the saucepan. Cover and cook for 5 minutes.

7 Spoon the casserole on to two plates or dishes. Fluff up the couscous with a fork, drain the peas and spoon on to the plates. Cool slightly before serving.

1 Preheat the oven to 180°C/ 350°F/Gas 4. Rinse the meat under cold water and pat dry. Trim away any fat and cut into small cubes. Chop the onion, remove the seeds and core from the peppers and cut into small cubes.

2 Heat the oil in a small frying pan or saucepan, add the beef and onion and fry gently until browned, stirring frequently.

3 Add the peppers and kidney beans, then stir in the flour, stock, tomato ketchup, Worcestershire sauce and a little salt and pepper if liked.

Lamb Stew

Serves 2

115g/4oz lamb fillet

¼ small onion

1 small carrot, about 50g/2oz

½ small parsnip, about 50g/2oz

1 small potato

5ml/1 tsp oil

150ml/¼ pint/⅔ cup lamb stock

pinch of dried rosemary

salt and pepper (optional)

crusty bread, to serve

1 Rinse the lamb under cold water and pat dry. Cut away any fat from the meat and cut into small cubes. Finely chop the onion, then dice the carrot and parsnip and cut the potato into slightly larger pieces.

2 Heat the oil in a medium-size saucepan, add the lamb and onion and fry gently until browned. Add the carrot, parsnip and potato and fry the lamb and vegetables for a further 3 minutes, stirring.

3 Add the lamb stock, dried rosemary and a little salt and pepper, if liked. Bring to the boil, cover and simmer for 35–40 minutes or until the meat is tender and moist.

4 Spoon the stew into shallow bowls and cool slightly before serving with crusty bread.

Mexican Mince

Serves 3–4

¼ small onion

1 strip red pepper

½ small courgette, about 50g/2oz

115g/4oz lean minced beef

1 small garlic clove, crushed

45ml/3 tbsp canned baked beans

45ml/3 tbsp beef stock

15ml/1 tbsp tomato ketchup

18 corn chips

25g/1oz/¼ cup grated Cheddar
   cheese

green salad, to serve

1 Finely chop the onion and dice the pepper and courgette.

2 Dry fry the onion and mince in a medium-size saucepan, stirring until browned all over.

3 Stir in the remaining ingredients and bring to the boil, stirring. Cover and simmer the mixture for 15 minutes, stirring occasionally.

4 Place the corn chips on plates, spoon on the mixture and sprinkle the grated cheese over the top. Serve with a green salad.

Lamb and Celery Casserole

Serves 2

115g/4oz lamb fillet

¼ onion

1 small carrot, about 50g/2oz

1 celery stick

25g/1oz button mushrooms

5ml/1 tsp oil

10ml/2 tsp plain flour

175ml/6fl oz/¾ cup lamb stock

bay leaf

salt and pepper (optional)

mashed potatoes and baby Brussels
   sprouts, to serve

1 Preheat the oven to 180°C/ 350°F/Gas 4. Rinse the lamb under cold water and pat dry, then trim off any fat and cut into small cubes. Chop the onion and carrot, rinse the celery and mushrooms, pat dry and slice thinly.

2 Heat the oil in a frying pan, add the lamb, onion and bay leaf and fry gently until the lamb is browned, stirring frequently. Add the remaining vegetables and fry for a further 3 minutes until they are softened and lightly brown.

VARIATION

For a more unusual flavour, substitute fennel for the celery. Its slight aniseed taste goes well with lamb.

3 Stir in the flour, then add the stock, and a little salt and pepper, if liked. Bring to the boil and then transfer to a casserole, cover and cook in the oven for 45 minutes or until the meat is tender.

4 Spoon the casserole on to plates discarding the bay leaf. Cool slightly then serve with mashed potatoes and tiny Brussels sprouts.

Shepherds' Pie

Serves 2

½ small onion
175g/6oz lean minced beef
10ml/2 tsp plain flour
30ml/2 tbsp tomato ketchup
150ml/¼ pint/⅔ cup beef stock
pinch of mixed herbs
slice swede, about 50g/2oz
½ small parsnip, about 50g/2oz
1 medium-sized potato, about 115g/ 4oz
10ml/2 tsp milk
15g/½oz/1 tbsp butter or margarine
½ carrot
40g/1½oz/3 tbsp frozen peas
salt and pepper (optional)

1 Preheat oven to 190°C/375°F/ Gas 5. Finely chop the onion, and place in a small saucepan with the mince and dry fry over a low heat, stirring, until the mince is evenly browned.

5 Spoon the mince into two 250ml/8fl oz/1 cup ovenproof dishes. Place the mashed vegetables on top fluffing them up with a fork. Dot with butter or margarine.

6 Place both the pies on a baking sheet and cook for about 25–30 minutes until browned on top and bubbly.

7 Peel and thinly slice the carrot lengthways. Stamp out shapes with petits fours cutters. Cook in a saucepan of boiling water with the peas for 5 minutes. Drain and serve with the shepherds' pies. Remember that baked pies are very hot when they come out of the oven. Always allow to cool slightly before serving to children.

2 Add the flour, stirring, then add the ketchup, stock, mixed herbs and seasoning, if liked. Bring to the boil, cover and simmer gently for 30 minutes, stirring occasionally.

3 Meanwhile, chop the swede, parsnip and potato and cook for 20 minutes until tender. Drain.

4 Mash with the milk and half of the butter or margarine.

Tuna Fish Cakes

Serves 2–3

1 large potato, about 225g/8oz
knob of butter or margarine
10ml/2 tsp milk
5ml/1 tsp lemon juice
100g/3½oz can tuna fish
40g/1½oz/3 tbsp frozen sweetcorn, defrosted
flour, for dusting
1 egg
60ml/4 tbsp ground almonds
50g/2oz green beans
½ carrot
6 frozen peas
15ml/1 tbsp oil
salt and pepper (optional)

1 Peel and cut the potato into chunks and then cook in a saucepan of boiling water for about 15 minutes until tender.

2 Drain the potato and mash with the butter or margarine, milk, lemon juice and a little salt and pepper, if liked. Drain the tuna fish and stir into the potato with the defrosted sweetcorn.

3 Divide the mixture into six and pat each portion into a fish shape with floured hands.

4 Beat the egg in a dish and place the ground almonds on a plate. Dip the fish cakes into the egg and then into the almonds making sure they are completely covered. Place on a floured plate and chill until ready to cook.

5 Trim the beans, peel and cut the carrot into sticks a little smaller than the beans. Cook in a pan of boiling water with the peas for about 5 minutes.

6 Meanwhile heat the oil in a frying pan, and fry the fish cakes for 5 minutes until golden brown and crisp, turning once.

7 Drain and arrange on serving plates with pea "eyes" and bean and carrot "pond weed". Cool slightly before serving.

Cheesy Fish Pies

Serves 2

1 medium-sized potato, about 150g/5oz
25g/1oz green cabbage
115g/4oz cod or hoki fillets
25g/1oz/2 tbsp frozen sweetcorn
150ml/¼ pint/⅔ cup milk
15ml/1 tbsp butter or margarine
15ml/1 tbsp plain flour
25g/1oz/¼ cup grated red Leicester cheese
5ml/1 tsp sesame seeds
carrots and mange tout, to serve

1 Peel and cut the potato into chunks and shred the cabbage. Cut any skin away from the fish fillets and rinse under cold water.

2 Bring a saucepan of water to the boil, add the potato and cook for 10 minutes. Add the cabbage and cook for a further 5 minutes until tender. Drain.

3 Meanwhile place the fish fillets, the sweetcorn and all but 10ml/2 tsp of the milk in a second saucepan. Bring to the boil then cover the saucepan and simmer very gently for 8–10 minutes until the fish flakes easily when pressed with a knife.

4 Strain the fish and sweetcorn, reserving the cooking liquid. Wash the pan then melt the butter or margarine in the pan. Stir in the flour then gradually add the reserved cooking liquid and bring to the boil, stirring until thickened and smooth.

5 Add the fish and sweetcorn with half of the grated cheese. Spoon into two small ovenproof dishes.

6 Mash the potato and cabbage with the remaining 10ml/2 tsp milk. Stir in half of the remaining cheese and spoon the mixture over the fish. Sprinkle with the sesame seeds and the remaining cheese.

7 Cook under a preheated grill until the topping is browned. Cool slightly before serving with vegetable fishes.

Surprise Haddock Parcels

Serves 2

| ½ small courgette, about 50g/2oz |
| 175g/6oz smoked haddock |
| 1 small tomato |
| knob of butter or margarine |
| pinch of dried mixed herbs |
| new potatoes and broccoli, to serve |

1 Preheat the oven to 200°C/
400°F/Gas 6. Tear off two pieces
of foil, then trim and thinly slice the
courgette and divide equally
between the two pieces of foil.

2 Cut the skin away from the fish,
remove any bones, cut into two
equal pieces and rinse under cold
water. Pat the haddock dry and place
on top of the courgettes.

3 Slice the tomato and arrange
slices on top of each piece of
haddock. Add a little butter or
margarine to each and sprinkle with
mixed herbs.

4 Wrap the foil around the fish and
seal the edges of each to make
two parcels, then place the parcels on
a baking sheet and cook in the oven
for 15–20 minutes depending on the
thickness of the fish.

5 To test for doneness, open up
one of the parcels and insert a
knife into the centre. If the fish flakes
easily then it is ready.

6 Cool slightly then arrange the
parcels on plates and serve with
new potatoes and broccoli.

Cowboy Bangers and Beans

Serves 2

3 chipolata sausages

¼ small onion

1 small carrot, about 50g/2oz

1 strip red pepper

5ml/1 tsp oil

200g/7oz can baked beans

10ml/2 tsp Worcestershire sauce

fingers of toast, to serve

1 Press the centre of each sausage, twist and cut in half to make two small sausages.

2 Finely chop the onion, then dice the carrot and the pepper, discarding the core and seeds.

3 Heat the oil in a frying pan, add the sausages and the chopped onion and fry until browned.

TIP
Check the beans towards the end of cooking, you may need to add a little extra water.

4 Add the remaining ingredients and stir in 30ml/2 tbsp water. Cover and cook for 15 minutes or until the carrot is cooked.

5 Spoon on to serving plates or into dishes, cool slightly and serve with fingers of toast.

Mini Toad-in-the-Hole

Serves 2

3 chipolata sausages

5ml/1 tsp oil

60ml/4 tbsp plain flour

1 egg

60ml/4 tbsp milk

salt

baked beans and green beans, to serve

1 Preheat the oven to 220°C/ 425°F/Gas 7. Press the centre of each sausage with your finger, twist and then cut in half. Brush two 10cm/4in Yorkshire pudding tins with oil. Add the sausages and cook for about 5 minutes.

2 Place the flour, egg and a pinch of salt in a bowl. Gradually whisk in the milk, beating until a smooth batter is formed.

3 Pour into the tins, quickly return to the oven and bake for 15 minutes until risen and golden.

4 Loosen with a knife and turn out on to serving plates. Cool slightly and serve with baked beans and steamed green beans.

Pork Hot-pot

Serves 2

175g/6oz lean pork
¼ small onion
5ml/1 tsp oil
5ml/1 tsp plain flour
150ml/¼ pint/⅔ cup chicken stock
40g/1½oz/3 tbsp frozen sweetcorn
pinch of dried sage
1 medium potato, about 150g/5oz
1 carrot, about 75g/3oz
knob of butter or margarine
salt and pepper (optional)
broccoli and Brussels sprouts, to serve

1 Preheat the oven to 180°C/ 350°F/Gas 4. Rinse the pork under cold water, pat dry, trim away any fat and cut into small cubes. Peel and finely chop the onion.

2 Heat the oil in a frying pan, add the cubed pork and onion and fry until golden brown, stirring.

3 Add in the flour and stir until blended, then add the sweetcorn, dried sage, stock and a little salt and pepper, if liked. Bring to the boil and then turn the mixture into a shallow ovenproof dish.

4 Peel and thinly slice the potato and carrot. Arrange slices so that they overlap on top of the pork mixture. Dot with butter or margarine. Cover with foil and cook in the oven for about 1 hour until the potatoes are tender.

5 Remove the foil and brown under the grill if liked. Spoon on to serving plates, cool slightly, then serve with steamed broccoli and tiny Brussels sprouts.

TIP
If you only have one child, make the hot-pots in two dishes. Cool one, cover with clear film and freeze for up to three months.

Pork and Lentil Casserole

Serves 2

175g/6oz boneless spare rib pork chop

¼ small onion

1 small carrot, about 50g/2oz

5ml/1 tsp oil

1 small garlic clove, crushed

25g/1oz red lentils

90ml/6 tbsp canned chopped tomatoes

90ml/6 tbsp chicken stock

salt and pepper (optional)

swede and peas, to serve

1 Preheat the oven to 180°C/ 350°F/Gas 4. Trim off any excess fat from the pork and cut in half. Finely chop the onion and dice the carrot.

2 Heat the oil in a frying pan, add the pork and onion and fry until the pork is browned on both sides.

3 Add the garlic, lentils and carrots and stir gently to mix.

4 Pour in the chopped tomatoes, stock and seasoning, if liked, and cook briefly to bring to the boil. Transfer to a casserole, cover and cook in the oven for 1¼ hours.

5 Spoon portions on to serving plates or shallow dishes and cool slightly. Serve with diced buttered swede and peas.

TIP
Teaching a child to use a knife and fork can be frustrating. Spare rib pork chops are wonderfully tender when casseroled and so very easy to cut with a child's knife.

Sticky Ribs and Apple Slaw

Serves 2

225g/8oz short pork ribs

10ml/2 tsp oil

10ml/2 tsp tomato ketchup

10ml/2 tsp Hoi sin sauce

1 medium potato, scrubbed but not peeled

knob of butter or margarine

For the Apple Slaw

½ carrot

½ eating apple

25g/1oz white cabbage

10ml/2 tsp sultanas

30ml/2 tbsp mayonnaise

carrot slices, tomato wedges and celery sticks, to serve

4 Meanwhile peel the carrot and peel, quarter and core the apple. Coarsely grate the apple and carrot and finely chop the cabbage.

5 Place in a bowl with the sultanas and mayonnaise and mix well.

6 Arrange the ribs on serving plates. Halve the baked potato and add a little butter or margarine to each half and serve with the pork ribs together with star-shaped carrot slices, celery sticks and tomato wedges and spoonfuls of coleslaw.

TIP
Check the temperature of the ribs before serving as they stay very hot for a surprisingly long time. Nothing will put a child off more than food that is very hot. Toddlers prefer their food to be lukewarm.

1 Preheat the oven to 200°C/ 400°F/Gas 6. Rinse the pork ribs under cold water, pat dry and put on a roasting rack set over a small roasting tin. Mix the oil, ketchup and Hoi sin sauce and brush over the ribs, reserving any extra mixture.

2 Pour a little boiling water into the base of the roasting tin. Prick the potato all over with a fork and then place in the oven with the spare ribs, preferably on the same shelf.

3 Cook for 1 hour, turning the pork ribs once during cooking and brushing with any of the remaining ketchup mixture.

Mini Cheese and Ham Tarts

Makes 12

For the Pastry

115g/4oz/1 cup plain flour

50g/2oz/4 tbsp sunflower margarine

For the Filling

50g/2oz/½ cup Cheddar cheese

2 slices wafer thin ham, chopped

75g/3oz/½ cup frozen sweetcorn

1 egg

120ml/4fl oz/½ cup milk

pinch of paprika

salt and pepper

carrot and cucumber sticks, to serve

1 Preheat the oven to 200°C/ 400°F/Gas 6. Place the flour in a bowl, add the margarine and rub in with fingertips until the mixture resembles fine breadcrumbs.

2 Stir in 20ml/4 tsp water and mix to make a smooth dough. Lightly knead and roll out thinly on a floured surface.

3 Stamp out twelve 7.5cm/3in circles with a fluted biscuit cutter, rerolling the pastry as necessary. Press into a bun tray.

TIP
Encourage children to eat more vegetables by serving them with a yogurt dip flavoured with tomato purée.

4 Grate the cheese, mix with the ham and sweetcorn and divide among the pastry cases.

5 Beat together the egg, milk, salt and pepper and pour into the tarts. Sprinkle with paprika.

6 Cook in the oven for 12–15 minutes until well risen and browned. Serve warm with carrot and cucumber sticks.

GOING GREEN

Getting children to eat more than a few frozen peas and the odd carrot can be an uphill battle. Encourage them to be a little more adventurous by mixing their favourite foods with some new vegetables.

Pick-up Sticks

Serves 2

5cm/2in piece of leek

25g/1oz green beans

1 strip red pepper

1 celery stick

25g/1oz bean sprouts

1 small carrot, about 50g/2oz

5ml/1 tsp oil

15ml/1 tbsp tomato ketchup

5ml/1 tsp soy sauce

pinch ground ginger

grilled sausages, to serve

1 Rinse the leek, beans, pepper, celery and bean sprouts. Peel the carrot. Halve any large beans and bean sprouts. Cut the remaining vegetables into thin strips.

2 Heat the oil in a frying pan, add all the vegetables except the bean sprouts and fry for 3 minutes, stirring all the time.

3 Add the bean sprouts, ketchup, soy sauce, ginger and 10ml/2 tsp water. Cook for a further 2 minutes, stirring until the vegetables are hot.

4 Spoon on to serving plates and leave to cool slightly. Serve with grilled sausages.

TIP
Don't overcook the vegetables. They should be quite crisp, and firm enough for your child to pick up.

Saucy Spinach Pancakes

Serves 2–3

50g/2oz fresh spinach, leaves only
50g/2oz plain flour
1 egg yolk
300ml/½ pint/1¼ cups milk
15ml/1 tbsp margarine
15ml/1 tbsp plain flour
25g/1oz/¼ cup grated red Leicester cheese
40g/1½oz wafer thin ham, chopped
40g/1½oz button mushrooms, thinly sliced
15ml/1 tbsp oil

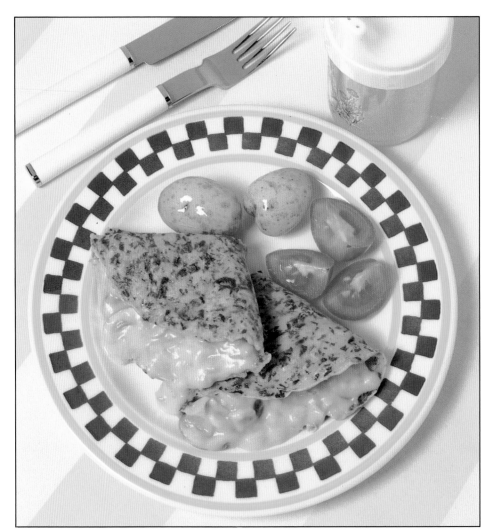

1 Wash the spinach leaves well in cold water and then place in a frying pan, set over a medium heat. Cover and cook gently for 2–3 minutes until the spinach has just wilted, stirring occasionally. Drain off any excess liquid and cool.

2 Put the flour, egg yolk and a little salt and pepper, if liked, into a bowl. Whisk in half of the milk to make a smooth batter. Finely chop the spinach and stir into the batter.

3 Melt the margarine in a saucepan, stir in the flour and then gradually stir in the remaining milk and bring to the boil, stirring continuously until smooth. Add the cheese, ham and mushrooms and stir to mix. Heat, cover and keep warm.

4 Heat a little oil in a frying pan, pour off excess then add 30ml/ 2 tbsp pancake batter, tilting the pan so that the batter covers the base. Cook for a few minutes until browned, then flip over and cook the other side until golden. Slide the pancake on to a plate and keep warm.

5 Continue making pancakes until all the batter is used up.

6 Fold the pancakes into quarters then spoon a little of the ham mixture into each one. Arrange the pancakes on plates and serve with tomato wedges and new potatoes.

TIP
If offering spinach to your child for the first time make sure that the filling includes foods that you know are liked. Omit or add ingredients as necessary.

Broccoli and Cauliflower Cheese

Serves 2

1 egg

75g/3oz broccoli

75g/3oz cauliflower

15g/½oz/1 tbsp margarine

15ml/1 tbsp plain flour

150ml/¼ pint/⅔ cup milk

40g/1½oz/⅓ cup grated red
Leicester cheese

½ tomato

salt and pepper (optional)

1 Put the egg in a small saucepan of cold water, bring to the boil and cook for about 10 minutes until the egg is hard-boiled.

2 Meanwhile cut the broccoli and cauliflower into florets and thinly slice the broccoli stalks. Cook in a saucepan of boiling water for about 8 minutes until just tender.

3 Drain the vegetables and dry the pan. Melt the margarine, stir in the flour then gradually mix in the milk and bring to the boil, stirring until thickened and smooth.

TIP
Making a face or fun pattern can be just enough to tempt a fussy eater to try something new.

4 Stir two-thirds of the cheese into the sauce together with a little seasoning, if liked. Reserve two of the broccoli florets and stir the remaining vegetables into the sauce.

5 Divide the mixture between two heat-resistant shallow dishes and sprinkle with the remaining cheese.

6 Place under a hot grill until golden brown and bubbling.

7 Make a face on each dish with broccoli florets for a nose, a halved tomato for a mouth and peeled and sliced hard-boiled egg for eyes. Cool slightly before serving.

Potato Boats

Serves 2

2 small baking potatoes
5cm/2in piece leek
25g/1oz button mushrooms
10ml/2 tsp oil
25g/1oz/2 tbsp frozen sweetcorn
15ml/1 tbsp milk
knob of butter
½ courgette, about 50g/2oz, grated
1 carrot, about 50g/2oz, grated
2 slices processed cheese
1 slice ham
salt and pepper (optional)

1 Preheat the oven to 200°C/ 400°F/Gas 6. Prick the potatoes with a fork and bake for 1 hour until soft. Alternatively, prick well and then microwave on a sheet of kitchen paper on High (full power) for 7–8 minutes.

2 Halve the leek lengthways, wash thoroughly to remove any grit and then slice thinly. Rinse the mushrooms, pat dry and thinly slice.

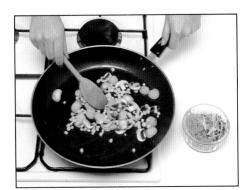

3 Heat 5ml/1 tsp oil in a frying pan and gently fry the leek, mushrooms and sweetcorn for about 3 minutes until softened, stirring frequently. Turn into a bowl and keep warm.

4 When the potatoes are cooked, cut in half and scoop the centres into the bowl with the leek and mushroom mixture. Add the milk, butter and a little salt and pepper if liked, and stir to mix. Pile the mixture back into the potato shells.

5 Reheat the remaining 5ml/1 tsp of oil and fry the grated courgette and carrot for 2 minutes until softened. Spoon on to two small plates and spread with a fork to cover the bases of the plates.

6 Arrange two potato halves on each plate. For sails, cut the cheese and ham into triangles and secure to potatoes with cocktail sticks. Cool slightly before serving.

Fat Cats

Serves 2

oil, for greasing

200g/7oz frozen puff pastry, defrosted

a little flour, for dusting

beaten egg, to glaze

50g/2oz broccoli

25g/1oz/2 tbsp frozen mixed vegetables

15ml/1 tbsp butter or margarine

15ml/1 tbsp plain flour

100ml/3½fl oz/½ cup milk

30ml/2 tbsp grated Cheddar cheese

a little mustard and cress, to garnish

1 Preheat the oven to 220°C/
425°F/Gas 7 and lightly brush a
baking sheet with a little oil. Roll out
the pastry thinly on a surface lightly
dusted with a little flour.

2 Using a shaped biscuit cutter,
stamp out four 13cm/5in cat
shapes. Place two cats on the baking
sheet and brush with egg.

3 Cut a large hole in the centre of
the two remaining cats and
gently place the shapes on top of the
other two cats.

VARIATION
Ring the changes by making this
recipe using different shaped biscuit
cutters to cut out the pastry shapes.
Get your child to choose his favourite.

4 Brush the tops with egg and
cook for 10 minutes until the
pastry is well risen and golden.

5 Meanwhile chop the broccoli
and cook in a small saucepan of
boiling water with the frozen
vegetables for 5 minutes. Drain.

6 Dry the pan and melt the butter
or margarine. Stir in the flour
and then gradually add the milk.
Bring to the boil, stirring all the time
until thickened and smooth.

7 Reserve two peas and two pieces
of carrot for garnish and then
stir the remaining vegetables into the
sauce with the grated cheese.

8 Enlarge the cavity in the centre
of each pastry cat by scooping
out a little of the pastry. Spoon in the
vegetable mixture and arrange on
two serving plates. Garnish with
halved peas for eyes, halved carrot
strips for whiskers and red pepper
noses. Add mustard and cress grass.
Cool slightly before serving.

Potato, Carrot and Courgette Rösti

Serves 2–4

1 small potato, about 115g/4oz
½ carrot, about 25g/1oz
½ courgette, about 25g/1oz
10ml/2 tsp sunflower oil
sausages and baked beans, to serve

1 Grate the potato, carrot and courgette into a bowl and mix together thoroughly.

2 Place several sheets of kitchen paper on a surface and put the vegetables on top. Cover with more kitchen paper and press down to soak up all the excess liquid.

3 Heat the oil in a frying pan and spoon the vegetables into the pan to form eight rounds. Flatten slightly with a fork and fry four of the rounds for 5 minutes, turning once until the potatoes are thoroughly cooked and the rösti is golden brown on both sides.

4 Lift out of the pan and cook the remaining mixture. Cool slightly and serve with grilled sausages and baked beans.

Veggie Burgers

Serves 2–4

1 large or 2 small potatoes, about 225g/8oz
1 carrot, about 50g/2oz
25g/1oz broccoli
25g/1oz Brussels sprouts
1 egg yolk
15ml/1 tbsp plain flour
15ml/1 tbsp freshly grated Parmesan cheese
15ml/1 tbsp oil
salt and pepper (optional)
canned spaghetti hoops, pieces of cucumber, strips of ham and tomato ketchup, to serve

1 Cut the potato and carrot into chunks and cook in boiling water for 15 minutes until tender.

2 Meanwhile, cut the broccoli into small florets, chop the stem finely and thinly slice the Brussels sprouts. Rinse under cold water then add to the potatoes and carrots for the last 5 minutes of cooking.

3 Drain the vegetables thoroughly and then mash together. Add the egg yolk and a little salt and pepper, if liked, then mix well.

4 Divide into four and shape into burgers with floured hands. Coat in flour and Parmesan cheese.

5 Heat the oil in a frying pan, add the burgers and fry for 5 minutes, turning once until golden brown. Cool slightly then serve with canned spaghetti hoops, strips of ham, a few cucumber wedges and a little tomato ketchup. Add a face with peas, carrot and cucumber.

TIP
To make a spider add cooked green bean legs, a red pepper mouth and yellow pepper eyes.

Vegetable Lasagne

Serves 2–3

¼ small onion
50g/2oz carrot
50g/2oz courgette
50g/2oz aubergine
25g/1oz button mushrooms
10ml/2 tsp oil
1 small garlic clove, crushed
225g/8oz can chopped tomatoes
pinch of mixed herbs
15ml/1 tbsp butter or margarine
15ml/1 tbsp plain flour
150ml/¼ pint/⅔ cup milk
60ml/4 tbsp grated cheese
3 sheets pre-cooked lasagne
salt and pepper
mixed salad, to serve

1 Finely chop the onion and carrot, and finely dice the courgette and aubergine. Wipe and thinly slice the mushrooms.

2 Heat the oil and fry the vegetables for 3 minutes until softened. Add the garlic, tomatoes and herbs, then bring to the boil, cover and simmer for 5 minutes.

3 Melt the butter or margarine in a saucepan, stir in the flour. Add the milk and bring to the boil, stirring, until thickened. Stir in half of the grated cheese and a little salt and pepper.

4 Preheat the oven to 180°C/ 350°F/Gas 4. Spoon one-third of the vegetable mixture into the base of an ovenproof dish, then add a little sauce. Add a slice of lasagne then cover with half of the remaining vegetable mixture and half the remaining sauce.

5 Add a second sheet of pasta and top with the remaining vegetable mixture. Add a third sheet of lasagne and top with the remaining cheese sauce. Sprinkle with the remaining cheese.

6 Cook for 50–60 minutes, checking after 30 minutes and covering loosely with foil if the topping is browning too quickly. Spoon on to serving plates and leave the lasagne to cool slightly. Serve with a little mixed salad.

Aubergine Bolognese

Serves 2

50g/2oz aubergine

1 strip red pepper

1 strip yellow pepper

5cm/2in piece of leek

1 carrot, about 50g/2oz

10ml/2 tsp oil

1 small garlic clove, crushed

25g/1oz/2 tbsp frozen sweetcorn

25g/1oz/2 tbsp red lentils

225g/8oz can chopped tomatoes

250ml/8fl oz/1 cup vegetable stock

pinch of dried herbs

50g/2oz dried pasta shapes

knob of butter or margarine

30ml/2 tbsp grated cheese (optional)

salt and pepper

1 Rinse the aubergine, peppers and leek, peel the carrot and then finely dice all the vegetables.

2 Heat the oil in a medium-sized saucepan, add the diced vegetables and gently fry for 3 minutes, stirring frequently, until they are slightly softened.

TIP
Sprinkle the diced aubergine with salt, leave to drain in a colander for 30 minutes, then rinse. This removes any bitter taste.

3 Add the garlic, sweetcorn, lentils, tomatoes, stock, herbs and a little salt and pepper.

4 Bring to the boil, cover and simmer for about 30 minutes, stirring occasionally and adding a little extra stock if necessary.

5 In the last 10 minutes of cooking, bring a pan of water to the boil and add the pasta. Cook for 10 minutes until tender.

6 Drain, toss in a little butter or margarine. Spoon on to plates and top with the aubergine bolognese. Sprinkle with cheese.

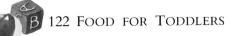
QUICK TEAS

I F YOU'VE HAD A DAY RUSHING AROUND, THEN RUSTLE UP THESE QUICK AND TASTY TODDLERS'
TEAS – THEY ALL COOK IN 10 MINUTES OR LESS. THERE IS A WIDE VARIETY OF RECIPES TO CHOOSE
FROM. REMEMBER THE IMPORTANCE OF FUN PRESENTATION, TO TEMPT YOUR TODDLER TO TRY NEW
FOODS.

Speedy Chicken Pie

Serves 2

1 celery stick

25g/1oz/2 tbsp frozen sweetcorn,
   defrosted

30ml/2 tbsp mayonnaise

2.5ml/½ tsp ground coriander

75g/3oz cold cooked chicken

½ small packet plain crisps

15ml/1 tbsp grated red Leicester
   cheese

salt and pepper (optional)

peas and broccoli, to serve

2 Spoon into a shallow ovenproof
dish and level the surface.

3 Roughly crush the crisps and
sprinkle over the chicken. Top
with the grated cheese and cook for
10 minutes until hot and bubbly.

4 Cool slightly then serve the pie
with peas and broccoli.

1 Preheat the oven to 220°C/
425°F/Gas 7. Rinse the celery,
slice thinly and place in a bowl with
the sweetcorn, mayonnaise, ground
coriander and a little salt and pepper,
if liked. Dice the chicken, add to the
bowl and mix well.

VARIATION
Mexican Chicken Pie
Replace the ground coriander with
ground cumin and replace the crisps
with about 30ml/2 tbsp crumbled
plain tortilla chips.

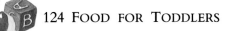

Skinny Dippers

Serves 2

150g/5oz boneless, skinless chicken breast

25g/1oz/¼ cup grated Cheddar cheese

50g/2oz/1 cup fresh breadcrumbs

15g/½oz/1 tbsp butter or margarine

115g/4oz frozen oven chips

½ small carrot, cut into thin strips

½ small courgette, cut into thin strips

45ml/3 tbsp tomato ketchup

1 Rinse the chicken under cold water and pat dry with kitchen paper. Cut into thin strips.

2 Mix the grated cheese and breadcrumbs on a plate. Melt the butter or margarine in a small saucepan or in a dish in the microwave on High (full power) for 20 seconds, then toss the chicken strips in the butter or margarine and roll in the breadcrumb mixture.

3 Arrange the chicken and chips on a foiled-lined baking sheet. Preheat the grill and bring a saucepan of water to the boil.

4 Grill the chicken for 6–8 minutes and the chips 8–10 minutes until both are well browned, turning once. When the chicken is ready, keep warm in a shallow dish while the chips finish cooking.

5 Cook the vegetables for 5 minutes in the pan of boiling water until tender.

6 Spoon the ketchup into two ramekins or egg cups and place in the centre of two serving plates. Drain the vegetables and divide the vegetables, chicken and chips between the two plates. Allow to cool slightly before dipping into ketchup.

TIP
Keep a supply of fresh breadcrumbs in a sealed plastic bag in the freezer. There is no need to defrost, just take out as much as you need and use from frozen.

Sweet and Sour Chicken

Serves 2

50g/2oz/¼ cup long grain white rice
1 carrot, about 50g/2oz
1 courgette, about 50g/2oz
2 skinless chicken thighs
10ml/2 tsp oil
25g/1oz/2 tbsp frozen peas
5ml/1 tsp cornflour
5ml/1 tsp soy sauce
10ml/2 tsp tomato ketchup
60ml/4 tbsp orange juice
1 egg, beaten

1 Cook the rice in boiling water for 8–10 minutes until tender.

2 Meanwhile, peel the carrot, trim the courgette and cut both into thin strips. Bone the chicken and cut into small chunks.

3 Heat 5ml/1 tsp of the oil in a frying pan, add the carrot, courgette, chicken and peas and fry for 5 minutes, stirring occasionally.

4 Blend the cornflour with the soy sauce and then stir into the pan together with the ketchup and orange juice. Cook gently, stirring all the time, until the sauce is glossy and has thickened.

TIP
Make the meal into an occasion and serve the food in Chinese bowls with Chinese spoons – chopsticks may be a little too tricky to manage. All children love the idea of eating in a restaurant with a parent to wait on them.

5 Drain the rice thoroughly. Add the remaining oil to the rice together with the beaten egg and cook over a gentle heat stirring until the egg has scrambled.

6 Spoon the rice and sweet and sour chicken on to serving plates and cool slightly before serving.

Ham and Tomato Scramble

Serves 2

| 2 slices ham |
| 1 tomato |
| 1 small strip yellow pepper |
| 2 eggs |
| 15ml/1 tbsp milk |
| 2 slices bread |
| a little butter |
| salt |

1 Finely chop the ham. Halve the tomato, scoop out and discard the seeds then chop into small dice. Finely chop the strip of pepper.

2 Beat the eggs and milk together and season with a little salt. Toast the bread lightly.

3 Heat a small knob of butter in a saucepan, add the eggs, ham, tomato and pepper and cook gently, stirring all the time until cooked to taste. Cool slightly.

4 Butter the toast and cut into shapes with small fancy-shaped biscuit cutters. Arrange on plates with the ham and tomato scramble.

TIP
If you don't have any special cutters then cut the toast into tiny triangles and squares with a knife.

Ham Salad Clown

Serves 2

| 2 slices ham |
| 1 cherry tomato |
| 2 slices apple |
| 1 slice cheese |
| 2 currants |
| 2 slices hard-boiled egg |
| a little mustard and cress |
| 2 long slices carrot |

TIP
Have fun varying the ingredients for the clown. Use cheese slices, radishes, peaches, raisins, lettuce and red pepper to change the appearance and features.

1 Cut two large rounds from the slices of ham using a biscuit cutter or the top of a glass or other container as a guide. Arrange on two plates and add a halved tomato for a nose and slice of apple for a mouth, trimming if needed.

2 Cut out small triangles or stars of cheese with a knife for eyes, place on the ham and add halved currants for eye balls.

3 Halve the egg slices and add to the face for ears. Snip the mustard and cress for hair and use snipped pieces of carrot for a ruff.

Spanish Omelette

Serves 2

2 slices wafer thin ham
1 strip red pepper
15ml/1 tbsp frozen peas
50g/2oz frozen oven chips
5ml/1 tsp oil
1 egg
salt and pepper (optional)
tomato wedges, to serve

1 Chop the ham and pepper. Mix the pepper and peas. Slice the oven chips.

2 Heat the oil in a non-stick frying pan, and fry the chips for 5 minutes, stirring, until lightly browned. Add the pepper and peas and cook, stirring, for a further 2 minutes. Stir in the chopped ham.

3 Beat together the egg, 10ml/ 2 tsp water and a little salt and pepper, if liked, and pour into the pan, tilting it so that the egg mixture covers the base evenly.

4 Cook over a medium-low heat for 2–3 minutes until the base of the omelette is set and browned. Loosen the edges and invert the pan on to a plate to turn out the omelette. Then slide the omelette back into the pan and cook the second side for a few more minutes until golden.

5 Cut the omelette into wedges, arrange on two plates and cool slightly. Serve with tomato wedges.

Saucy Ham Pasta

Serves 2

50g/2oz dried pasta shapes

50g/2oz/½ cup frozen mixed vegetables

30ml/2 tbsp margarine

30ml/2 tbsp plain flour

150ml/¼ pint/⅔ cup milk

50g/2oz/½ cup grated red Leicester or Cheddar cheese

2 slices ham, chopped

salt and pepper

1 Cook the pasta in a saucepan of boiling water for 5 minutes. Add vegetables and cook for 5 more minutes until pasta is tender. Drain.

2 Melt the margarine in a medium-sized pan and stir in the flour. Gradually add the milk and bring to the boil, stirring, until the sauce is thickened and smooth.

3 Stir two-thirds of the grated cheese into the sauce and add the drained pasta and vegetables, the ham and a little salt and pepper.

4 Spoon into two shallow dishes and sprinkle with the remaining cheese. Cool slightly if necessary.

TIP
This recipe also works well if you use a 100g/3½oz can tuna, drained, in place of the ham. You could serve the ham and vegetable sauce with rice, if you prefer.

Quickie Kebabs

Serves 2–3

1 tomato

3 slices ham

½ small yellow pepper

6 button mushrooms

6 cocktail sausages

10ml/2 tsp tomato ketchup

10ml/2 tsp oil

canned spaghetti, to serve

1 Preheat the grill. Cut the tomato into six wedges and cut each slice of ham into two strips. Roll up each strip. Cut the pepper into six chunks, discarding any seeds. Wipe the mushrooms.

2 Make six kebabs by threading a tomato wedge, a ham roll, a piece of pepper, a mushroom, and a sausage on to six cocktail sticks.

TIP
Use two rashers of rindless bacon, if preferred. Halve and roll up and use in place of the ham.

3 Line a grill pan with foil and arrange the kebabs on top. Blend the ketchup and oil and brush over the kebabs. Grill for 10 minutes, turning once and brushing with the juices until the vegetables are browned and the sausages are thoroughly cooked.

4 Cool slightly then arrange on plates with canned spaghetti.

Sausage Wrappers

Serves 2

4 slices ham

10ml/2 tsp tomato relish or barbecue sauce

4 sausages

baked beans and grilled potato shapes, to serve

1 Spread one side of each slice of ham with relish or sauce.

2 Cut each piece of ham into three thin strips and then wrap each sausage in three strips securing them in place with cocktail sticks.

3 Grill for 10 minutes, turning several times until the ham is browned and crisp.

4 Cool slightly then remove the cocktail sticks and serve the sausage wrappers with baked beans and grilled potato shapes.

TIP
Use four pieces of rindless streaky bacon instead of ham, if preferred.

Corned Beef Hash

Serves 2

1 potato, about 175g/6oz

10ml/2 tsp oil

50g/2oz green cabbage

115g/4oz corned beef

pinch of turmeric

15ml/1 tbsp tomato ketchup

hard-boiled egg slices, to garnish

1 Dice the potato and cook in a saucepan of boiling water for 3–4 minutes until softened. Drain.

2 Heat the oil in a medium-sized frying pan, add the diced potato and fry for 3 minutes until golden.

3 Meanwhile, chop the cabbage and dice the corned beef.

5 Stir in the ketchup and spoon on to two plates. Cool slightly before serving. Garnish with the hard-boiled egg slices.

4 Add the cabbage and turmeric to the pan with the potatoes and cook for 2 minutes. Stir in the corned beef and cook for 2 minutes.

TIP
The hash can be garnished with tomato wedges, if liked.

Cannibal Necklaces

Serves 2

45ml/3 tbsp stuffing mix

60ml/4 tbsp boiling water

115g/4oz lean minced beef

5ml/1 tsp oil

½ carrot

1 strip red pepper

1 strip green pepper

a little tomato ketchup

1 Put the stuffing mix in a bowl and pour over the boiling water. Set aside for 5 minutes to soak.

2 Stir the mince into the stuffing mix and shape into 10 small balls with floured hands.

3 Preheat the grill. Arrange the meat balls on a piece of foil on top of the grill pan and brush lightly with a little oil. Grill for 7–8 minutes, until well browned, turning once during cooking.

4 Meanwhile thinly slice the carrot and cut the pepper into chunks, discarding the core and seeds.

5 Arrange the meat balls around the bottom edge of two serving plates. Leave spaces in between.

TIP
If you're feeling adventurous, liven up simple teas by piping the child's initials on to the edge of the plate, the appropriate number for their age or even a short word like "hello".

6 Place carrot and pieces of red and green pepper between each meat ball and complete with a line and bow of ketchup for necklace strings, straight from the bottle, or pipe the ketchup if preferred.

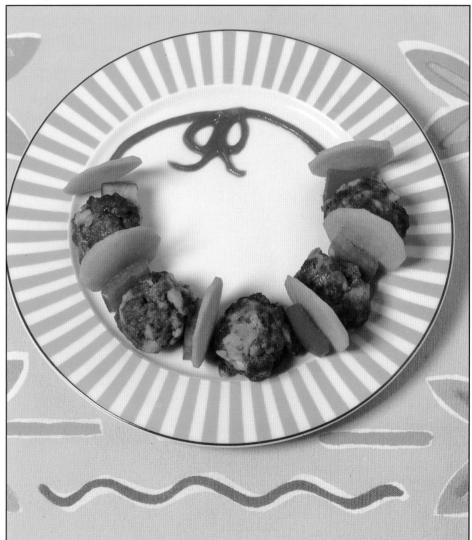

Beef and Mushroom Burgers

Serves 2

¼ small onion
25g/1oz button mushrooms
115g/4oz lean minced beef
115g/4oz frozen oven chips
2 burger buns
10ml/2 tsp tomato ketchup
1 tomato
salt and pepper (optional)

1 Finely chop the onion, wipe and chop the mushrooms. Place the mince in a mixing bowl, add the onion and mushrooms and a little salt and pepper, if liked, and mix together thoroughly. Alternatively blend the mixture in a processor.

2 With floured hands shape two 7.5cm/3in burgers or press the mixture into a plastic burger press or upturned pastry cutter.

3 Preheat the grill. Tear off two large pieces of foil. Fold up the edges and place on a grill pan. Put the burgers on one piece and the chips on the other.

4 Cook the burgers and chips for 10 minutes turning the food once. Remove from the grill rack and keep warm. Split the burger buns in half and toast on one side only.

5 Spread the bases of the buns with ketchup, slice the tomato and place on the buns. Top each with a burger and the second bun half. Cut in half and arrange on serving plates with the chips. Cool slightly if necessary before serving.

Four Fast Fishes

Serves 2

115g/4oz hoki or cod fillet
½ egg, beaten
60ml/4 tbsp fresh breadcrumbs
10ml/2 tsp sesame seeds
10ml/2 tsp oil
15ml/1 tbsp frozen peas
4 frozen sweetcorn niblets
1 carrot
canned spaghetti rings, to serve

1 Cut away and discard any skin from the fish and rinse. Pat dry and cut into four pieces.

2 Put the egg in a saucer and place the breadcrumbs and sesame seeds on a plate. Dip pieces of fish in egg and then in breadcrumb mixture to coat the fish.

3 Heat the oil in a frying pan, add the fish and fry for 4–5 minutes, turning once, until the fish pieces are golden brown and cooked.

4 Meanwhile cook the peas and sweetcorn in a saucepan of boiling water for 5 minutes. Cut the carrot into long thin slices and then cut out fin and tail shapes and tiny triangles for mouths.

5 Arrange the pieces of fish on two plates with the carrot decorations, sweetcorn for eyes and peas for bubbles. Serve with warmed canned spaghetti rings.

TIP
You can freeze the uncooked breaded portions to provide a quick meal at a later date when you are pushed for time. Freeze them on a tray and then wrap them well to prevent the odour tainting other food in the freezer.

Tuna Risotto

Serves 2

5ml/1 tsp oil

¼ onion, finely chopped

50g/2oz long grain white rice

50g/2oz frozen mixed vegetables

1 small garlic clove, crushed

10ml/2 tsp tomato ketchup

100g/3½oz can tuna fish in water

salt and pepper (optional)

1 Heat the oil in a small saucepan and fry the chopped onion for about 3 minutes until softened.

2 Add the rice, mixed vegetables, garlic, tomato ketchup and 250ml/8fl oz/1 cup water and a little salt and pepper, if liked.

TIP
If liked use cold leftover cooked chicken, lamb or beef in place of the tuna.

3 Bring to the boil and simmer uncovered for 10 minutes. Drain the tuna and add to the rice mixture, stirring to mix. Cook for 3–4 minutes, stirring occasionally, until the water has been absorbed by the rice and the rice is tender.

4 Spoon on to plates and cool slightly before serving.

Fish Finger Log Cabins

Serves 2

4 frozen fishfingers

25g/1oz green cabbage

8 mange-tout

2 frozen peas

1 strip green pepper

1 strip red pepper

1 Grill the fishfingers for 10 minutes, turning once until golden. Meanwhile finely shred the cabbage and cook in boiling water for 3 minutes. Add the mange-tout and peas and cook for a further 2 minutes. Drain well.

2 Arrange two fishfingers side by side on each plate. Trim the mange-tout and use them to make a roof, slightly overlapping the edges of the fishfingers.

VARIATION
Sausage Log Cabin
Use four grilled cocktail chipolata sausages for each cabin. Make the roof from green beans and use shredded spinach for the grass.

3 Cut four windows from the green pepper and two doors from the red pepper and add to the log cabins, using peas as door handles. Arrange the shredded cabbage to look like grass.

Toast Toppers

ALL CHILDREN, EVEN THE FUSSIEST OF DINERS, LOVE BREAD AND THERE IS NO QUICKER CONVENIENCE FOOD. RING THE CHANGES WITH THESE SUPER-SPEEDY SNACKS.

Shape Sorters

Serves 2

4 slices bread

butter or margarine, for spreading

30ml/2 tbsp smooth peanut butter

50g/2oz/½ cup grated Cheddar cheese

4 cherry tomatoes

3 slices cucumber

VARIATION
Pizza Shape Sorters
Spread the shapes with tomato ketchup. Chop a tomato finely, and sprinkle over the shapes, then add some grated cheese. Grill until bubbly and golden.

1 Toast the bread lightly on both sides and remove crusts. Stamp out shapes using square, star, triangle and round.

2 Spread the shapes with butter or margarine and then peanut butter. Place the shapes on a baking sheet and sprinkle with cheese.

3 Grill until the cheese is bubbly. Cool slightly, arrange on a plate and serve with tomato wedges and quartered cucumber slices.

Happy Families

Serves 2

3 slices bread

butter or margarine, for spreading

3 slices processed cheese

2 slices ham

a little mustard and cress

1 strip red pepper

½ carrot

small pieces of cucumber

1 Stamp out men and women shapes from the bread using small cutters. Spread with a little butter or margarine.

2 Stamp out cheese dresses using the woman cutter and trimming off the head. Press on to three of the bodies. Cut out cheese jumpers and ham trousers and braces. Add to the remaining shapes.

3 Snip off the leaves from mustard and cress and use for eyes. Cut tiny red pepper mouths and make necklaces and bow ties from the carrot and cucumber using flower cutters. Arrange on plates.

Eggy Bread Butterflies

Serves 2

4 small broccoli florets
8 peas
1 small carrot
1 slice red Leicester or Cheddar cheese
2 slices ham
2 slices bread
1 egg
10ml/2 tsp milk
5ml/1 tsp sunflower oil
a little tomato ketchup

1 Cook the broccoli florets and the peas in a saucepan of boiling water for 5 minutes. Drain well.

2 For each butterfly, cut four thin slices of carrot and cut into flower shapes with a petits four cutter. Cut out four small squares from the cheese.

3 Cut four thin strips from the rest of the carrot for antennae. Roll up each piece of ham and arrange in the middle of two serving plates, to make the two butterfly bodies.

4 Cut butterfly wings from the bread using a small knife.

TIP
Vary the ingredients for butterfly decorations. Make a body from a grilled sausage if preferred.

5 Beat together the egg and milk and dip the bread in to coat both sides thoroughly. Heat the oil in a medium-sized frying pan and fry the bread until golden on both sides.

6 Assemble the butterfly, using the eggy bread for the wings and decorating with the carrot, cheese, broccoli and peas. Use a blob of ketchup for the head.

Tuna Flowers

Serves 2–3

6 thin slices bread

25g/1oz butter, plus extra if
necessary

10ml/2 tsp plain flour

75ml/5 tbsp milk

60ml/4 tbsp grated red Leicester or
Cheddar cheese

100g/3½oz can tuna fish, drained

50g/2oz/4 tbsp frozen mixed
vegetables, defrosted

½ carrot

6 slices cucumber, halved

a little mustard and cress

salt and pepper (optional)

1 Preheat the oven to 200°C/
400°F/Gas 6. Cut out six flower
shapes from the bread using a 9cm/
3½in scalloped biscuit cutter. Flatten
each piece slightly with a rolling pin.

4 Stir the flour into the remaining
butter (you should have about
10ml/2 tsp left). Gradually stir in the
milk and bring to the boil, stirring
until the sauce is thick and smooth.

5 Stir in 30ml/3 tbsp of the cheese,
the tuna, the mixed vegetables
and a little salt and pepper, if liked.

6 Heat through and then spoon
into the baked bread cups and
sprinkle with remaining cheese.

7 Arrange the tuna cups on
serving plates. Cut the carrot
into thin strips for flower stems and
add to the plate with halved
cucumber slices for leaves and
mustard and cress for grass.

2 Melt the butter in a saucepan or
microwave. Brush a little over
one side of each piece of bread and
then press the bread, buttered side
downwards, into sections of a bun
tray. Brush the second side of bread
with a little more butter.

3 Bake in the oven for about 10–
12 minutes until crisp and
golden around the edges.

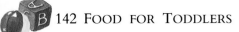

Noughts and Crosses

Serves 2

8 green beans

¼ red pepper

6 slices snack pepperami sausage

2 slices bread

butter or margarine, for spreading

115g/4oz Cheddar cheese

TIP
To vary the topping, use thin strips of carrot or ham for the grid, sliced sausage, frankfurter or carrot for the noughts, carrot, green pepper or cucumber for the crosses.

1 Trim the beans, thinly slice the pepper, discarding any seeds and thinly slice the pepperami sausage.

2 Cook the beans in boiling water for 5 minutes. Toast the bread lightly on both sides and spread with butter or margarine. Thinly slice the cheese and place on the toast.

3 Drain the beans and arrange four on each piece of toast to form a grid. Add crosses made from pepper strips and noughts from pieces of the pepperami sausage.

4 Grill the toasts until the cheese is bubbly. Arrange on plates and cool slightly before serving.

Stripy Cheese on Toast

Serves 2

2 slices bread

butter or margarine, for spreading

50g/2oz Cheddar cheese

50g/2oz red Leicester cheese

2 cherry tomatoes, to serve

1 Toast the bread lightly on both sides then spread each slice with butter or margarine.

2 Thinly slice the cheese and then cut into strips about 2.5cm/1in wide. Arrange alternate coloured cheese strips over the toast and grill the toasts until bubbly.

3 Cool slightly, then cut into squares, arrange on plates and serve with cherry tomato wedges.

TIP
If your child likes Marmite add a thin scraping underneath the cheese slices. You could also spread ketchup or peanut butter for a surprise flavour.

Speedy Sausage Rolls

Makes 18

8 slices multi-grain white bread

225g/8oz cocktail sausages

40g/1½oz/3 tbsp butter or
   sunflower margarine

carrot and cucumber sticks, to serve

1 Preheat the oven to 190°C/
375°F/Gas 5. Trim the crusts off
the bread and cut into slices a little
smaller than the sausages.

2 Wrap each piece of bread around
a sausage and secure with a
halved cocktail stick. Place the
sausage rolls on a baking sheet.

3 Melt the butter or margarine in a
small saucepan or in the
microwave and brush over the
prepared sausage rolls.

4 Bake in the oven for 15 minutes
until browned. Cool slightly
and remove the cocktail sticks.
Arrange on a plate and serve with
carrot and cucumber sticks.

TIP
If liked spread a little tomato relish
or ketchup over the bread before
wrapping around the sausages to
give a sharper flavour. Spread the
bread with a little mild, prepared
mustard if you child likes it. If the
bread is thickly cut, flatten it
slightly with a rolling pin, before
wrapping around the sausages.

Pizza Clock

Serves 3–4

20cm/8in ready-made pizza base

45ml/3 tbsp tomato ketchup or pizza
  sauce

2 tomatoes

75g/3oz/¾ cup grated cheese

pinch of dried marjoram

1 green pepper

1 large carrot

1 thick slice ham

1 Preheat oven to 220°C/425°F/
Gas 7. Place the pizza base on a
baking sheet and spread with
ketchup or pizza sauce. Chop the
tomatoes and scatter over the pizza
with the cheese and marjoram.

2 Place directly on an oven shelf
and bake for 12 minutes, until
the cheese is bubbly. (Place a baking
tray on the shelf below the pizza to
catch any drips of cheese.)

3 Meanwhile halve the pepper, cut
away the core and seeds and
stamp out the numbers 3, 6, 9 and 12
with small number cutters. Peel and
thinly cut the carrot lengthways and
stamp out the numbers 1, 2, 4, 5, 7,
8, 10 and 11. Arrange on the pizza to
form a clock face.

4 Cut out a carrot circle. Cut two
clock hands, each about 7.5cm/
3in long from the ham. Arrange on
the pizza with the round of carrot.

5 Place the pizza clock on to a
serving plate and arrange the
numbers around the edge. Cool the
pizza clock slightly before cutting
into wedges and serving.

TIP
If preferred, make a smaller
version of this using half a toasted
muffin. Top as above and grill
until the cheese melts. Add ham
hands and small pieces of carrot
to mark the numbers.

Spotty Sandwiches

Serves 2

1 hard-boiled egg
30ml/2 tbsp mayonnaise
2 slices white bread
2 slices brown bread
a little mustard and cress
½ small carrot
a little shredded lettuce

1 Peel and finely chop the egg, place in a small bowl and blend well with the mayonnaise.

2 Stamp out giraffe shapes from the brown and white bread using an animal biscuit cutter.

3 Cut tiny rounds from each shape using the end of a metal piping tube and then replace the rounds with opposite coloured bread circles.

4 Spread the egg mayonnaise over half of the shapes and top with the remaining shapes. Arrange on plates with snipped mustard and cress for grass and shaped carrot slices for flowers.

Sandwich Snails

Serves 2

1 strip red pepper
small piece cucumber
15ml/1 tbsp frozen sweetcorn, defrosted
25g/1oz/¼ cup grated Cheddar cheese
15ml/1 tbsp mayonnaise
1 slice bread
2 cooked sausages

1 Cut away any seeds from the pepper and cut out four small squares for the snails' eyes and cut four strips of cucumber for their antennae. Finely chop the remaining pepper and cucumber and mix with the sweetcorn, cheese and mayonnaise. Place in a bowl.

2 Trim the crusts off the bread, cut in half and overlap two short edges together to make a long strip. Flatten slightly with a rolling pin so that the bread bonds together.

VARIATION
For pasta snails, use large shell pasta instead of the bread and stuff with the sweetcorn mixture.

3 Spread the bread with the cheese mixture and roll up tightly. Squeeze together then cut in half crossways to make two rounds.

4 Arrange each slice, cut side uppermost, on two serving plates. Arrange the sausages for bodies, and use the cucumber strips for antennae and the red pepper squares for the eyes.

EASY PEASY PUDS

With a young family to feed, puddings need to be quick, light and taste good without the kids realizing they're healthy too! Remember to keep sugar to a minimum.

Fruit Fondue

Serves 2

150g/5oz tub ready-to-serve low-fat custard

25g/1oz milk chocolate

1 eating apple

1 banana

1 satsuma

a few strawberries or seedless grapes

1 Pour the custard into a saucepan, add the chocolate and heat, stirring all the time until the chocolate has melted. Cool slightly.

2 Quarter the apple, core and cut into bite-sized pieces, slice the banana and break the satsuma into segments. Hull the strawberries and wash the grapes, if using.

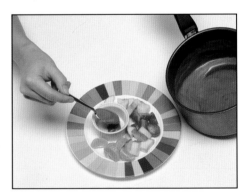

3 Arrange the fruit on two small plates, pour the custard into two small dishes and place on the plates. The fruit can be dipped into the custard using either a fork or fingers.

TIP
Add the chocolate to a tub of custard and microwave on Full Power (100%) for 1½ minutes or until the chocolate has melted. Stir and spoon into dishes. Cool slightly.

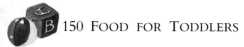

Strawberry Ice Cream

Makes 900ml/1½ pint/3¾ cups

300ml/½ pint/1¼ cups double cream

425g/15oz can custard

450g/1lb strawberries

teddy bear wafers, to decorate

strawberries, to decorate

1 Whip the cream until softly peaking then fold in the custard.

2 Hull the strawberries and then rinse and pat dry. Process to make a smooth purée, then press through a sieve into the cream and custard. Fold together.

3 Pour the mixture into a plastic tub and freeze the ice cream for 6–7 hours until half frozen.

4 Beat the ice cream with a fork or process in a food blender until smooth, then return the tub to the freezer and freeze until solid.

5 Remove the ice cream from the freezer 10 minutes before serving so that it can soften slightly. Scoop into serving bowls and decorate each with teddy bear wafers and extra fruit such as strawberries.

VARIATIONS
Strawberry Ripple Ice Cream
Purée and sieve an extra 250g/9oz strawberries and sweeten with 30ml/ 2 tbsp icing sugar. Swirl this into the half-frozen ice cream at Step 4 and then freeze until solid.

Apricot and Chocolate Chip Ice Cream
Whisk 300ml/½ pint/1¼ cups double cream, and fold in 425g/15oz can custard. Drain and purée the contents of a 425g/15oz can apricot slices in natural juice and stir into the cream with the finely grated rind of 1 orange. Pour into a plastic tub, freeze until mushy and then beat well. Stir in 100g/3½oz packet chocolate dots and freeze again until solid. Scoop into serving dishes and decorate the ice cream with orange segments and wafers, if liked.

Raspberry Sorbet

Makes: 900ml/1½ pints/3¾ cups

10ml/2 tsp powdered gelatine

600ml/1 pint/2½ cups water

225g/8oz/1¼ cups caster sugar

675g/1½lb raspberries, hulled

grated rind and juice of ½ lemon

1 Put 30ml/2 tbsp water in a cup, sprinkle the gelatine over and set aside for a few minutes to soak.

2 Place the water and sugar in a saucepan and heat, stirring occasionally until the sugar has completely dissolved.

3 Bring to the boil and boil rapidly for 3 minutes. Remove from the heat, add the gelatine mixture to the syrup and stir until completely dissolved. Leave to cool.

4 Liquidize or process the raspberries to a smooth purée then press through a sieve into the syrup. Stir in lemon rind and juice.

5 Pour into a plastic tub and freeze for 6–7 hours or until the mixture is half frozen.

6 Beat the sorbet with a fork or transfer to a food processor and process until smooth. Return to the freezer and freeze until solid.

7 Remove the sorbet from the freezer 10 minutes before serving to soften slightly, then scoop into dishes with a melon baller or small teaspoon.

VARIATION
Summer Fruit Sorbet

Follow the recipe up to Step 3. Put a 500g/1¼lb pack of frozen summer fruits into a second saucepan. Add 60ml/4 tbsp water, cover and cook for 5 minutes until soft, then purée and sieve, add to the syrup and continue as above.

Yogurt Lollies

Makes 6

150g/5oz tub strawberry yogurt

150ml/¼ pint/⅔ cup milk

10ml/2 tsp strawberry milkshake powder

1 Mix the yogurt, milk and milkshake powder together.

2 Pour the mixture into six small plastic lolly moulds. Add the lolly handles and freeze overnight.

TIP
Store lollies for up to a week in the freezer. Make sure they are tightly covered as they can pick up other flavours in the freezer.

3 Dip the lolly moulds into hot water, count to 15, then flex handles and remove. Serve at once.

Jolly Jellies

Serves 4

150g/5oz packet strawberry jelly

2 ripe plums

175g/6oz fromage frais or Greek yogurt

4 Dolly Mixtures

10ml/2 tsp sugar or chocolate strands

1 Cut the jelly into pieces. Place in a bowl and pour over 150ml/ ¼ pint/⅔ cup boiling water. Stir until dissolved then set aside to cool.

2 Halve the plums, cut away the stones and reserve four thin slices. Chop the remaining fruit and divide among four small dishes.

TIP
If you have a fussy eater who hates bits, finely chop or purée the plums before adding to the jelly so that the child doesn't know it's not just jelly!

3 Stir the fromage frais into the jelly and pour into the dishes. Chill in the refrigerator until set.

4 Decorate with sliced plums for mouths, halved dolly mixtures for the eyes and sugar or chocolate sugar strands for hair.

Pancakes

Serves 2–3

50g/2oz/⅓ cup plain flour

1 egg

150ml/¼ pint/⅔ cup milk

15ml/1 tbsp sunflower oil

For the filling

1 banana

1 orange

2–3 scoops ice cream

a little maple syrup

1 Sift the flour into a bowl, add the egg and gradually whisk in the milk to form a smooth batter. Whisk in 5ml/1 tsp of the oil.

2 To make the filling, slice the banana thinly or in chunks. Cut the peel away from the orange with a serrated knife, then cut the orange into segments.

3 Heat a little of the remaining oil in medium-sized non-stick pan, pour off any excess oil and add 30ml/2 tbsp of the batter. Tilt the pan to evenly coat the pan and cook for a couple of minutes until the pancake is set and the underside is golden.

4 Loosen the edges with a knife then toss the pancake or turn with a knife. Brown the other side and then slide out on to a plate. Fold in four and keep warm.

5 Cook the rest of the batter in the same way until you have made 6 pancakes. Place two on each plate.

6 Spoon a little fruit into each pancake and arrange on serving plates. Top with the remaining fruit, a scoop of ice cream and pour over a little maple syrup. Serve at once.

Traffic Light Sundaes

Serves 6

½ packet lime jelly

½ packet orange jelly

½ packet strawberry jelly

2 kiwi fruit

275g/10oz can mandarin oranges

6 scoops vanilla ice cream, to serve

12 strawberries to decorate

4 Add a little kiwi fruit and continue making layers using the orange jelly and mandarins and topping with the strawberry jelly.

5 Add half the strawberries, top with a scoop of ice cream and decorate with the remaining strawberries. Serve immediately.

1 Make up each jelly in a separate bowl with boiling water according to the instructions on the packet. Cool, then transfer to the fridge and allow to set.

2 Peel and slice the kiwi fruit, hull and rinse the strawberries and cut in half. Drain the mandarins.

3 Chop all of the jellies and divide the green jelly equally among six sundae glasses.

TIP
This is a great recipe for a party tea – simple but ever popular. For smaller numbers of children, halve the recipe to make three. Or for tiny children make up half-size sundaes in plastic cups.

Cheat's Trifle

Serves 2

2 slices Swiss roll

20ml/4 tsp orange juice

1 mandarin orange

50g/2oz strawberries

150g/5oz tub ready-to-serve custard

10ml/2 tsp Greek yogurt

2 sugar flowers, to decorate

TIP
Use 150ml/¼ pint/⅔ cup leftover custard if you have it or make custard with custard powder and 150ml/¼ pint/⅔ cup milk.

1 Put a slice of Swiss roll in the base of two ramekin dishes and spoon the orange juice over the top. Peel the mandarin orange and divide the segments between the dishes.

2 Hull, rinse and chop the strawberries. Place in dishes.

3 Spoon the custard over the strawberries, top with yogurt and decorate with sugar flowers.

Baked Bananas

Serves 2

2 medium bananas

2 small scoops ice cream

1 Preheat the oven to 180°C/ 350°F/Gas 4. Separate the unpeeled bananas and put on a baking sheet. Cook for 10 minutes until the skins have blackened and the bananas feel quite soft.

2 Hold the banana in a tea cloth, make a slit along the length of the banana and peel off the skin. Peel the second banana.

3 Slice and arrange each as a ring on a plate. Place a scoop of ice cream in the centre of each plate.

TIP
For an adult version, slit the banana and spoon in a teaspoon or two of coffee cream liqueur, eat out of the skin with a teaspoon.

QUICK CAKES AND BAKES THE KIDS CAN MAKE

COOKING IS FUN AND THE EARLIER YOU LEARN THE BETTER FUN IT IS. EVEN THE FADDIEST EATER CAN BE AN ENTHUSIASTIC COOK, AND HELPING TO DECIDE WHAT TO COOK FOR TEA CAN MAKE A CHILD MORE WILLING TO SIT DOWN WITH THE FAMILY AND HAND ROUND THEIR HOMEMADE GOODIES. LEARNING TO WEIGH OUT INGREDIENTS, TO MIX, SPREAD AND SPOON OUT, ALL HELPS WITH CO-ORDINATION AND ENCOURAGES A BASIC INTEREST AND LOVE OF FOOD.

Getting ready
- Find a large apron or cover the child's clothes with an old adult-sized shirt with the sleeves cut down.
- Always wash hands before you start to cook.

- Choose a sturdy chair for your child to stand on next to the work top or kitchen table. Or put a large cloth on the floor, set scales, bowls, ingredients etc out, and prepare food sitting down.

- Make it clear to your child that only the adult opens the oven door and touches saucepans on the cooker.
- Keep knives and scissors out of the way; provide blunt, round-ended scissors if required.

Orange and Apple Rockies

Makes 24

oil, for greasing
115g/4oz/½ cup sunflower margarine
225g/8oz/2 cups self-raising flour
1 large eating apple
50g/2oz ready-to-eat dried apricots
grated rind of 1 small orange
75g/3oz/⅓ cup demerara sugar
1 egg
15ml/1 tbsp milk
apple slices, to serve

1 Preheat the oven to 190°C/375°F/ Gas 5 and brush two baking sheets with a little oil. Rub the margarine into the flour with your fingertips until the mixture resembles fine breadcrumbs.

2 Peel, core and finely chop the apple, chop the apricots and stir into the flour mixture with the sultanas and orange rind. Reserve 30ml/2 tbsp of the sugar and stir the rest into the mixture.

3 Beat the egg and milk, add to the flour mixture and mix until just beginning to bind together.

4 Drop spoonfuls, well spaced apart on to the baking sheet. Sprinkle with the reserved sugar and bake in the oven for 12–15 minutes. Transfer to a serving plate and serve warm or cold with apple slices.

TIP
Freeze any leftover rockies in a plastic bag for up to three months.

Date Crunch

Makes 24 pieces

225g/8oz packet sweetmeal biscuits
75g/3oz stoned dates
75g/3oz/⅓ cup butter
30ml/2 tbsp golden syrup
75g/3oz sultanas
150g/5oz milk or dark chocolate

1 Line an 18cm/7in shallow tin with foil. Put the biscuits in a plastic bag and crush roughly with a rolling pin. Finely chop the dates.

2 Gently heat the butter and syrup in a small saucepan until the butter has melted.

TIP
For an alternative topping drizzle 75g/3oz melted white and 75g/3oz melted dark chocolate over the biscuit to give random squiggly lines. Chill until set.

3 Stir in the crushed biscuits, the dates and sultanas and mix well. Spoon into the tin, press flat with the back of a spoon and chill for 1 hour.

4 Break the chocolate into a bowl, melt over hot water, and then spoon over the biscuit mixture spreading evenly with a palette knife. Chill until set.

5 Lift the foil out of the tin and peel away. Cut the biscuit into 24 pieces and arrange on a plate.

Chocolate Dominoes

Makes 16

oil, for greasing

175g/6oz/¾ cup soft margarine

175g/6oz/⅞ cup caster sugar

150g/5oz/⅔ cup self-raising flour

25g/1oz cocoa powder, sifted

3 eggs

For the Topping

175g/6oz/¾ cup butter, softened

25g/1oz cocoa powder

300g/11oz/3 cups icing sugar

a few liquorice strips and 115g/4oz packet M & M's, for decoration

1 Preheat the oven to 180°C/350°F/ Gas 4. Lightly brush an 18 × 28cm/7 × 11in baking tin with a little oil and line the base of the tin with greaseproof paper.

2 Put all the cake ingredients in a bowl and beat until smooth.

3 Spoon into the tin and level the surface with a palette knife.

4 Bake in the oven for 30 minutes, or until the cake springs back when pressed with the fingertips.

5 Cool in the tin for 5 minutes, then loosen the edges with a knife and turn out on to a wire rack. Peel off the paper and allow the cake to cool.

6 Turn the cake on to a chopping board and cut into 16 bars.

7 To make the topping, place the butter in a bowl, sift in the cocoa and icing sugar and beat until smooth. Spread the topping evenly over the cakes with a palette knife.

8 Add a strip of liquorice to each cake, decorate with M & M's for domino dots and arrange the cakes on a serving plate.

VARIATION
Traffic Light Cakes
Makes 16
To make Traffic Light Cakes omit the cocoa and add an extra 25g/1oz/3 tbsp flour. Omit the cocoa from the icing and add an extra 25g/1oz/3 tbsp icing sugar and flavour with 2.5ml/½ tsp vanilla essence. Spread over the cakes and decorate with eight halved red, yellow and green glacé cherries to look like traffic lights. Arrange the cakes on a serving plate.

Marshmallow Krispie Cakes

Makes 45

oil, for greasing
250g/9oz bag toffees
50g/2oz/4 tbsp butter
45ml/3 tbsp milk
115g/4oz marshmallows
175g/6oz Rice Krispies

1 Lightly brush a 20 × 33cm/8 × 13in roasting tin with a little oil. Put the toffees, butter and milk in a saucepan and heat gently, stirring until the toffees have melted.

2 Add the marshmallows and cereal and stir until well mixed and the marshmallows have melted.

3 Spoon into the tin, level the surface and leave to set. Cut into squares, put into paper cases and serve.

Mini Muffins

Makes 24

200g/7oz/1½ cups plain flour
10ml/2 tsp baking powder
50g/2oz/¼ cup soft light brown sugar
150ml/¼ pint/⅔ cup milk
1 egg, beaten
50g/2oz/4 tbsp butter or margarine, melted
50g/2oz glacé cherries
50g/2oz ready-to-eat dried apricots
2.5ml/½ tsp vanilla essence

1 Preheat the oven to 220°C/425°F/Gas 7 and place 24 petits fours cases in the sections of two petits fours, or mini muffin tins.

TIP
For older children spoon the mixture into 12 medium-sized muffin cases. Muffins are best served warm from the oven. If they don't get eaten straight away, they can be frozen for up to three months.

2 Place the flour, baking powder and sugar in a bowl and add the milk, egg and melted butter or margarine and stir thoroughly until the mixture is smooth.

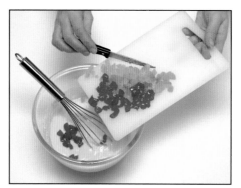

3 Chop the cherries and apricots and stir into the muffin mixture with the vanilla essence.

4 Spoon the muffin mixture into the paper cases so they are about three-quarters full.

5 Cook for 10–12 minutes until well risen and browned. If you have just one tin cook in two batches.

VARIATIONS
Chocolate Chip Muffins
Substitute 25g/1oz cocoa powder for 25g/1oz/2 tbsp flour. Omit the cherries, apricots and vanilla and add 50g/2oz white and 50g/2oz plain chocolate dots.

Orange and Banana Muffins
Substitute 2 small mashed bananas for 60ml/2fl oz/¼ cup milk. Omit the cherries, apricot and vanilla and add 15ml/1 tbsp grated orange rind.

Cup Cake Faces

Makes 12

115g/4oz/⅔ cup sunflower margarine
115g/4oz/⅔ cup caster sugar
115g/4oz/1 cup self-raising flour
2 eggs
For the Topping
50g/2oz/¼ cup butter
115g/4oz/1 cup icing sugar
pink food colouring
115g/4oz packet M & M's
2 red liquorice bootlaces
12 Dolly Mixtures
75g/3oz plain chocolate

1 Preheat the oven to 180°C/350°F/Gas 4. Place 12 paper cake cases in the sections of a bun tray.

2 Put all the cake ingredients into a bowl and beat until smooth.

3 Divide the cake mixture among the cases and cook for 12–15 minutes until well risen and the cakes spring back when pressed with a fingertip. Leave to cool.

4 Meanwhile make the topping: beat the butter in a bowl, sift in the icing sugar and beat the mixture until smooth. Stir in a little pink food colouring.

5 Spread the icing over the cakes. Add M & M eyes, short pieces of liquorice for mouths and a dolly mixture nose.

6 Break the chocolate into pieces, melt in a bowl over a saucepan of gently simmering water and then spoon into a greaseproof paper piping bag. Snip off the tip and pipe hair, eye balls, glasses and moustaches on to the cakes.

7 Carefully arrange in a single layer on a serving plate and allow the icing to set before serving.

VARIATION
Alphabet Cakes
Make up a half quantity of cake mixture as above and spoon into 24 mini muffin or petits fours cases. Put into sections of a mini muffin or petits fours tin or arrange on a baking sheet close together and cook for 8–10 minutes then cool. Blend 225g/8oz/2 cups sifted icing sugar with 30ml/2 tbsp water until smooth. Add a little water if necessary to make a thick spoonable icing. Spoon 30ml/2 tbsp into a piping bag fitted with a small writing tube. Spoon half the remaining icing into a separate bowl and colour pink. Colour the remaining icing blue. Spoon the icing over the cakes, smooth the surface and pipe on letters of the alphabet. Leave to set.

Gingerbread People

Makes 24

oil, for greasing
225g/8oz/2 cups plain flour
5ml/1 tsp ground ginger
1.5ml/¼ tsp ground cinnamon
7.5ml/1½ tsp bicarbonate of soda
50g/2oz/4 tbsp sunflower margarine
115g/4oz/⅔ cup soft light brown sugar
45ml/3 tbsp golden syrup
30ml/2 tbsp milk
75g/3oz dark chocolate
2 packets M & M's

1 Brush two baking sheets with a little oil. Sift the flour, spices and bicarbonate of soda into a bowl.

2 Place the margarine, sugar and syrup in a saucepan and heat until the margarine has melted.

3 Remove from heat and stir in the flour mixture and milk. Mix to a firm dough, chill for 30 minutes.

TIP
Chocolate decorations soften biscuits, so eat on the day or decorate as many biscuits as you will eat and store the rest in a tin for up to four days. For a party, decorate people with clothes cut from coloured ready-to-roll icing.

4 Preheat the oven to 160°C/ 325°F/Gas 3. Knead the dough lightly and roll out on a floured surface. Cut out gingerbread men and women with 9cm/3½in cutters. Place on the baking sheets, reroll the trimmings, stamp out nine gingerbread people and continue until all the dough is used.

5 Cook for 10 minutes until golden and then set aside to cool and harden a little on the trays. Loosen while still warm.

6 Break the chocolate into a bowl and melt over hot water, then spoon a little chocolate over the gingerbread men for trousers. Place on the baking tray to set.

7 Spoon the remaining chocolate into a piping bag fitted with a small writing tube and pipe faces on the gingerbread people and some swirls for petticoats on the women. Pipe two dots on all the people for buttons and stick on M & M's. Leave to set before serving.

Bread Animals

Makes 15

oil, for greasing
2 × 280g/10oz packets white bread mix
a few currants
½ small red pepper
1 small carrot
1 egg

1 Brush two large baking sheets with a little oil. Put the bread mixes in a large bowl and make up as directed on the packet with warm water.

2 Knead on a lightly floured surface for 5 minutes until the dough is smooth and elastic. Return the dough to the bowl, cover with oiled clear film and leave in a warm place for ¾–1 hour until it has doubled in size.

3 Preheat the oven to 220°C/425°F/Gas 7. Knead the dough again for 5 minutes and then divide into five pieces.

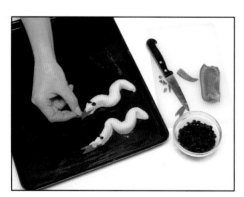

4 To make snakes, take one piece of dough, cut into three and shape each into a 15cm/6in snake, making a slit in one end for the mouth. Twist the snakes on the baking sheet. Insert two currants for eyes. Cut out a thin strip of pepper, cutting a triangle at one end for the forked tongue.

5 For hedgehogs, take another piece of dough and cut into three. Shape each into an oval about 6cm/2½in long. Place on the baking sheet and add currant eyes and a red pepper nose. Snip the dough with scissors to make the prickly spines.

6 For the mice, take a third piece of dough and cut into four pieces. Shape three pieces into ovals each about 6cm/2½in long and place on the baking sheet. Shape tiny rounds of dough for ears and wiggly tails from the fourth piece of dough. Press onto the mice bodies and use the currants for eyes.

7 Cut small strips of carrot and use for whiskers.

TIP
Give a portion of the prepared dough to your children, with some chopped dried fruits and allow them to create their very own Bread Animals.

8 For the crocodiles, cut another piece of dough into three. Take a small piece off each and reserve. Shape the large pieces into 10cm/4in long sausages. Make slits for the mouths and wedge open with crumpled foil. Add currant eyes. Shape the spare dough into feet and press into position. Make criss-cross cuts on the backs.

9 For rabbits, take the final piece of dough and cut into three. Take a small piece off each for tails. Roll the remaining pieces of dough into thick sausages 18cm/7in long. Loop the dough and twist twice to form the body and head of rabbit. Use the rest for tails.

10 Cover the shapes with oiled clear film and leave in a warm place for 10–15 minutes. Brush with beaten egg and cook for 10–12 minutes until golden.

11 Serve warm or cold split and filled with ham or cheese.

Cheesy Shapes

Makes 15

oil, for greasing

350g/12oz/3 cups self-raising flour

pinch of salt

115g/4oz/½ cup sunflower margarine

115g/4oz Cheddar cheese

2 eggs, beaten

60ml/4 tbsp milk

10ml/2 tsp sesame seeds

10ml/2 tsp poppy seeds

1 Preheat the oven to 220°C/ 425°F/Gas 7.

2 Place the flour and salt in a bowl, add the margarine and rub in with your fingertips or an electric mixer until the mixture resembles fine breadcrumbs.

3 Grate the cheese, reserve 30ml/ 2 tbsp and stir the rest into the flour. Add three-quarters of the beaten eggs and milk to the flour and mix to a soft dough.

4 Knead the dough lightly and roll out thickly on a surface that has been dusted with flour.

5 Stamp out numbers with 7cm/3in cutters and arrange well spaced apart on two baking sheets. Reroll trimmings and stamp out more shapes to use up the pastry.

6 Brush the tops of the numbers with the reserved egg. Sprinkle five of the numbers with sesame seeds, five with poppy seeds and the remainder with grated cheese.

7 Cook for 12–15 minutes until well risen and browned. Cool slightly then arrange the Cheesy Shapes on a plate and serve warm.

Marmite and Cheese Whirls

Makes 16

oil, for greasing

250g/9oz frozen puff pastry, defrosted

flour, for dusting

2.5ml/½ tsp Marmite

1 egg, beaten

50g/2oz red Leicester or Cheddar cheese, grated

carrot and cucumber sticks, to serve

1 Preheat the oven to 220°C/ 425°F/Gas 7 and brush a large baking sheet with a little oil.

2 Roll out the pastry on a floured surface to a large rectangle, about 35.5 × 25cm/14 × 10in.

3 Spread the pastry with Marmite, leaving a 1cm/½in border. Brush the edges of the pastry with egg and sprinkle the cheese to cover the Marmite.

TIP
Omit the Marmite and use peanut butter if preferred. If the shapes become a little squashed when sliced, reform into rounds by opening out the layers with the end of a knife.

4 Roll the pastry up quite tightly like a Swiss roll, starting from a longer edge. Brush the outside of the pastry with beaten egg.

5 Cut the roll into thick slices and place on the baking sheet.

6 Cook for 12–15 minutes until the pastry is well risen and golden. Arrange on a serving plate and serve warm or cold with carrot and cucumber sticks.

FAMILY MEALS

Eating together as a family takes on a new dimension as your family grows and there's a baby, fussy toddler and Mum and Dad to feed together. Rather than attempting to cook three different meals or to cook one very simple meal you know the children will like, opt instead to cook three meals from one basic set of ingredients; a simple baby dinner, eye-catching meal for even the fussiest of toddlers and a spicy dinner for the grown-ups.

The recipes are aimed at a baby aged nine months and over, a toddler or small child aged eighteen months to four years and two adults.

Eating Together

Family meal times should be a pleasure but they can all too often turn into a battleground. Whatever family rules you have about table manners it's important that all the family knows about them and that you are consistent. What matters to some families may not be important to you. If you want your children to stay at the table until everyone has finished, make sure all the family understands this. Some parents may feel it's more relaxing if the children leave the table once they have finished, leaving the adults to eat the rest of their meal in relative peace. Whatever you decide, stick to it, don't be brow beaten by well-meaning grandparents or friends.

Try to eat together as a family at

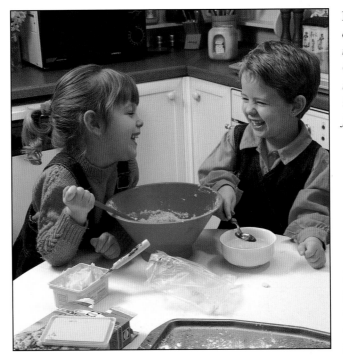

Left: *Part of the fun of eating together is sharing the preparation, too. Children love helping in the kitchen, and this involves them in the meal from the very start.*

Below: *A relaxed but polite atmosphere will enhance enjoyment and consequently encourage good eating habits.*

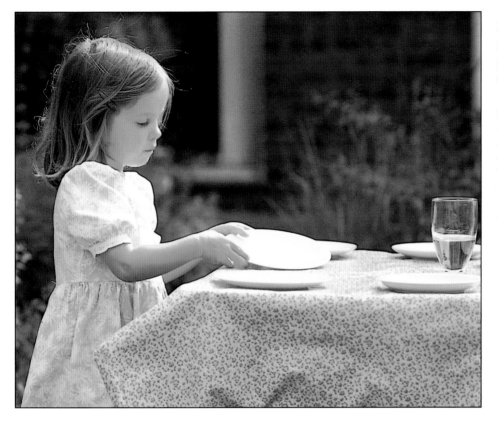

Similarly, beware of tiny hands reaching out from the highchair to grab a mug of hot coffee or snatch at a sharp knife.

Offer a variety of foods at each meal, some foods you know your toddler and baby will like and foods that you like too so that everyone is happy. Offer very tiny portions of foods that are new or ones that your child is not very keen on and encourage your child to have at least one mouthful.

Encourage baby to feed himself with easy-to-pick-up finger foods. This gives the adults a chance to eat their food too. Don't worry about the mess until you get to the end of the meal.

For added protection when your toddler is eating at the table, use a wipe-clean place mat and cover the seat of a dining chair with a towel or teatowel. Better still buy a thin padded seat cover that is removable and machine washable but will tie on to the seat securely.

Children cannot bear to eat foods that are too hot, not just because they may burn their mouths, but because of the frustration. Not being able to eat when the food is there and

least once a day, even if you don't all eat the same food, so that your toddler can learn how to behave by watching the rest of the family. Explain to other members of the family that you are all setting the baby an example – a great way to make everyone pull their socks up, whatever their age.

It is never too early to encourage children to help: laying the table can become quite a game, especially if dolly or teddy has a place set too. Passing plates, bread and salt and pepper can be perilous to begin with but with a little practice becomes second nature. Transform a dull wet Monday tea into a special occasion with a few flowers or candles (well out of reach of very tiny children) and pretty table mats and paper napkins for added decoration.

Try to avoid using a tablecloth with very young children as they can pull the cloth and everything with it on to the floor and themselves, with appalling consequences if there's a hot teapot or hot casserole dish.

Above: Laying the table is another task that children delight in, and another way to make them feel part of the family mealtime.

Below: Even if the child is too young to have exactly the same food, sharing the table is important.

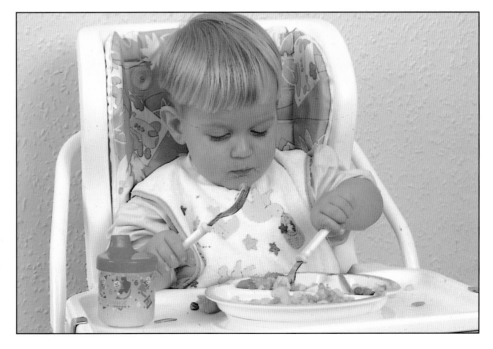

they are hungry can lead to great outbursts of temper. Many children actually prefer their food to be just lukewarm. Cool broccoli quickly by rinsing with a little cold water. Spoon hot casseroles on to a large plate so they cool quickly and always test the temperature of foods before serving to a child.

TABLE MANNERS

Toddlers can be incredibly messy, but try not to be too fussy and just wipe sticky hands and faces at the end of the meal. Enjoyment is the key. If your child is tucking into her meal with enthusiasm rather than style, then that is the most important part at the beginning – table manners will come as your child becomes more experienced and adept with a knife and fork.

Be understanding and flexible, small children have a lot to learn when they begin to join in with family meals. An active toddler has to learn how to sit still – quite an art in itself – how to hold a knife and fork and how to drink from a cup

Below and below right: Never forget that food and eating are meant to be fun – don't discipline the child just for the sake of it, and don't impose adult rules too quickly.

and somehow watch what everyone else is doing and join in too.

The baby has to adapt to sitting up to the table in his highchair and waiting for an adult to offer him a spoonful of food. Not surprisingly there can be a few tantrums and accidents, not to mention mess. Try not to worry. Offer a few finger foods after a bowl of minced foods so that the baby can feed himself, giving you a chance to finish your own meal and tidy up.

Above: *Good manners and sharing provide the perfect atmosphere for good eating – and will aid digestion, too!*

Left: *Unusual and varied environments, and the different types of food that go with them, provide huge additional pleasure, and will also help to familiarize your child with situations they will encounter later.*

TIPS

● Offer cubes of cheese at the end of a meal to help counteract the potentially harmful effects of any sugary foods eaten.

● Try to encourage children to eat more fruit. Cutting it into small pieces and arranging it on a plate can prove very inviting.

● Encourage children of all ages to drink full-fat milk, either cold, warm or flavoured, as it is a valuable source of the fat-soluble vitamins A and D and the important mineral calcium, vital for healthy bones and teeth.

● If you reheat baby food in the microwave, make sure you stir it thoroughly and leave it to stand for a couple of minutes so any hot spots can even out. Always check the temperature before serving.

● Always make sure a baby is well strapped into a highchair and never leave children unattended while eating in case of accidents.

● Children love the novelty of eating somewhere different. If it's a nice day, why not have a picnic in the local park. If eating outside, make food up separately.

● Snacks can play a vitally important part in a young child's diet as their growth rate is so high it can be difficult to provide sufficient calories and protein at mealtimes alone.

● Make sure you co-ordinate main meals and snacks so that you serve different foods and so that the snacks won't take the edge off the child's appetite for the main meal of the day.

● Try to avoid sweets or cakes and fatty crisps.

● Offer slices of fresh fruit, a few raisins or dried apricots, squares of cheese, a fruit yogurt or milky drink, marmite or smooth peanut butter on toast.

● Make food fun and allow your child to choose where they eat the snack, e.g. in the camp in the garden or at the swings.

MEATY MAIN MEALS

Trying to please all the family all of the time can be a bit of a tall order, especially when trying to cook tasty meals on a budget. Try these delicious new ways with quick-to-cook mince and chops, plus a speedy stir fry, or slow-cook Beef Bourgignon, Osso Bucco pork or Lamb hot-pot.

Mediterranean Lamb

3 lamb chump chops
350g/12oz courgettes
½ yellow pepper
½ red pepper
3 tomatoes
1 garlic clove, crushed
15ml/1 tbsp clear honey
few sprigs of fresh rosemary, plus extra to garnish
15ml/1 tbsp olive oil
200g/7oz can baked beans
salt and freshly ground black pepper
crusty bread, to serve

2 Season two of the chops for the adults with garlic, honey, rosemary and salt and pepper, and drizzle oil over the vegetables.

3 Cook under a hot grill for 12–14 minutes, turning once, until the lamb is well browned and cooked through and the vegetables are browned.

5 Chop or process the remaining lamb with four slices of courgette, two small pieces of pepper, two peeled tomato quarters and 15–30ml/1–2 tbsp of baked beans, adding a little boiled water if too dry. Spoon into a dish for the baby and test the temperature of the children's food before serving.

6 For the adult's portions, discard the cooked rosemary. Spoon the pan juices over the chops and garnish with fresh rosemary. Serve with crusty bread.

1 Rinse the chops under cold water, pat dry, trim off fat and place in the base of a grill pan. Trim and slice the courgettes, cut away the core and seeds from the peppers and then rinse and cut into chunky pieces. Rinse and cut the tomatoes into quarters and arrange the vegetables around the lamb.

4 Warm the baked beans in a small saucepan. Drain and transfer the unseasoned chop to a chopping board and cut away the bone and fat. Thinly slice half the meat for the toddler and arrange on a plate with a few of the vegetables and 30–45ml/ 2–3 tbsp of the baked beans.

TIP
Lamb varies hugely in price throughout the year. Depending on the season and price you may prefer to use lamb cutlets or loin chops. Allow two chops per adult and reduce the cooking time slightly as these chops are smaller. Do not give honey to young children. Use redcurrant jelly in place of honey for baby and adults if preferred.

Lamb Hot-pot

350g/12oz lamb fillet

1 onion

1 carrot

175g/6oz swede

15ml/1 tbsp sunflower oil

30ml/2 tbsp plain flour

450ml/¾ pint/1⅞ cups lamb stock

15ml/1 tbsp fresh sage or 1.5ml/
¼ tsp dried

50g/2oz black pudding (optional)

½ dessert apple

275g/10oz potatoes

15g/½oz/1 tbsp butter

225g/8oz Brussels sprouts

salt and freshly ground black pepper

1 Preheat the oven to 180°C/
350°F/Gas 4. Rinse the lamb
under cold water, pat dry, trim away
any fat and then slice thinly. Peel and
chop the onion, carrot and swede.

2 Heat the oil in a large frying pan
and fry the lamb, turning until
browned on both sides. Lift the lamb
out of the pan, draining off any
excess oil and transfer one-third to a
small 600ml/1 pint/2½ cup casserole
dish for the children and the rest to a
1.2 litre/2 pint/5 cup casserole dish
for the adults.

3 Add the vegetables to the pan
and fry for 5 minutes, stirring
until lightly browned.

4 Stir in the flour, then add the
stock and sage. Bring to the
boil, stirring, then divide between
the two casserole dishes.

5 Peel and chop the black pudding
if using, core, peel and chop the
apple and add both to the larger
casserole dish with a little seasoning.

6 Thinly slice the potatoes and
arrange overlapping slices over
both casserole dishes. Dot with
butter and season the larger dish.

7 Cover and cook in the oven for
1¼ hours. For a brown topping,
remove the lid and grill for a few
minutes at the end of cooking until
browned. Cook the Brussels sprouts
in boiling water for 8–10 minutes
until tender and drain.

8 Chop or process half the hot-pot
from the small casserole with a
few sprouts for the baby, adding
extra gravy if needed until the
desired consistency is reached.
Spoon into a baby dish.

9 Spoon the remaining child's
hotpot on to a plate, add a few
sprouts and cut up any large pieces.
Test the temperature of the
children's food before serving.

10 Spoon the hotpot for the
adults on to serving plates
and serve with Brussels sprouts.

TIP
Traditionally neck or scrag end of
lamb would have been used for
making a hotpot. This cut does
require very long slow cooking
and can be fatty with lots of bones
so not ideal for children. Fillet of
lamb is very lean, with very little
waste and makes a tasty and
healthier alternative.

Beef Korma

350g/12oz lean minced beef

1 onion, chopped

1 carrot, chopped

1 garlic clove, crushed

400g/14oz can tomatoes

pinch of dried mixed herbs

25g/1oz pasta shapes

50g/2oz creamed coconut

50g/2oz button mushrooms

50g/2oz fresh spinach leaves

15ml/1 tbsp hot curry paste

salt and freshly ground black pepper

boiled rice, warm naan bread and a
little grated Cheddar cheese
(optional), to serve

1 Dry fry the mince and onion in a
medium-sized saucepan, stirring
until the beef is browned.

2 Add the carrot, garlic, tomatoes
and herbs, bring to the boil,
stirring and then cover and simmer
for about 30 minutes, stirring
occasionally.

3 Cook the pasta in a small
saucepan of boiling water for 10
minutes until tender. Drain.

4 Meanwhile place the coconut in
a small bowl, add 120ml/4fl oz/
½ cup of boiling water and stir until
dissolved. Wipe and slice
mushrooms and wash and drain
spinach, discarding any large stalks.

5 Transfer one-third of the mince
to another saucepan. Stir the
coconut mixture, curry paste and
salt and pepper into the remaining
mince and cook for about 5 minutes,
stirring.

6 Mash or process one-third of the
pasta and reserved mince
mixture to the desired consistency
for baby and spoon into a small dish.

7 Spoon the remaining pasta and
reserved mince into a small bowl
for the older child.

8 Stir the mushrooms and spinach
into the curried mince and cook
for 3–4 minutes until the spinach has
just wilted. Spoon on to warmed
serving plates for the adults and
serve with boiled rice and warmed
naan bread. Sprinkle the toddler's
portion with a little cheese, if liked.
Test the temperature of the
children's food before serving.

TIP
Weigh spinach after it has been
picked over and stalks removed or,
if you're short of time, buy ready
prepared spinach. If you can't get
creamed coconut, use 120ml/
4fl oz/½ cup coconut milk instead,
or soak 25g/1oz/1 cup desiccated
coconut in 150ml/¼ pint/⅔ cup
boiling water for 30 minutes then
strain and use the liquid.

Bobotie with Baked Potatoes and Broccoli

3 medium baking potatoes

1 onion, chopped

350g/12oz lean minced beef

1 garlic clove, crushed

10ml/2 tsp mild curry paste

10ml/2 tsp wine vinegar

90ml/6 tbsp fresh breadcrumbs

15ml/1 tbsp tomato purée

25g/1oz sultanas

15ml/1 tbsp mango chutney

1 medium banana, sliced

2 eggs

20ml/4 tsp turmeric

120ml/4fl oz/½ cup skimmed milk

4 small bay leaves

225g/8oz broccoli, cut into florets

30ml/2 tbsp fromage frais or Greek yogurt

200g/7oz can baked beans

salt and freshly ground black pepper

1 Preheat the oven to 180°C/ 350°F/Gas 4. Scrub the potatoes, insert a skewer into each and bake for 1½ hours until tender.

2 Place the chopped onion and 225g/8oz of the beef in a saucepan and dry fry, until browned all over, stirring frequently.

3 Add the garlic and curry paste, stir well and cook for 1 minute, then remove from the heat and stir in the vinegar, 60ml/4 tbsp of the breadcrumbs, the tomato purée, sultanas and a little salt and pepper.

TIP
Serve any leftover adult portions cold with salad.

4 Chop up any large pieces of mango chutney and stir into the meat mixture with the banana slices. Spoon into a 900ml/1½ pint/3¾ cup ovenproof dish and press into an even layer with the back of a spoon.

5 Place the dish on a baking sheet, cover loosely with foil and cook for 20 minutes.

6 Meanwhile mix the remaining beef with the remaining breadcrumbs, then beat the eggs together and stir 15ml/1 tbsp into the meat. Make eight small meatballs about the size of a grape for the baby. Form the remaining beef into a 7.5cm/3in burger using an upturned biscuit cutter as a mould.

7 Blend the turmeric, milk and a little salt and pepper with the remaining eggs. Remove the cover from the Bobotie, and lay the bay leaves over the meat.

8 Pour the egg mixture over. Return to the oven for a further 30 minutes until well risen and set.

9 When the adults' portion is ready, heat the grill and cook the burger and meatballs until browned, turning once. The burger will take 8–10 minutes, while the meatballs will take about 5 minutes.

10 Cook the broccoli in boiling water until tender and drain.

11 Cut the Bobotie for the adults into wedges and serve with jacket potatoes topped with fromage frais and broccoli.

12 Serve the toddler's burger with half a potato, warmed baked beans and a few broccoli florets. Serve the baby's meatballs with chunky pieces of peeled potato and broccoli. Spoon a few baked beans into a small dish for baby. Test the temperature of the food before serving to the children.

Moussaka

1 onion, chopped

350g/12oz minced lamb

400g/14oz can tomatoes

1 bay leaf

1 medium aubergine, sliced

2 medium potatoes

1 medium courgette, sliced

30ml/2 tbsp olive oil

2.5ml/½ tsp grated nutmeg

2.5ml/½ tsp ground cinnamon

2 garlic cloves, crushed

salt and freshly ground black pepper

For the Sauce

30ml/2 tbsp sunflower margarine

30ml/2 tbsp plain flour

200ml/7fl oz/1 cup milk

pinch of grated nutmeg

15ml/1 tbsp freshly grated Parmesan cheese

20ml/4 tsp fresh breadcrumbs

3 Slice the potatoes thinly and cook in boiling water for 3 minutes. Add the courgette and cook for 2 minutes until tender.

4 Remove most of the slices with a slotted spoon and place in a colander, leaving just enough for the baby portion. Cook these for 2–3 minutes more until soft, then drain. Rinse the vegetables and drain well.

5 Rinse the salt off the aubergine and pat dry. Heat the oil in a frying pan and fry the aubergines until browned on both sides. Drain.

6 Spoon 45ml/3 tbsp of the mince mixture into a bowl with the baby vegetables and chop or purée to the desired consistency.

7 Spoon 60ml/4 tbsp of the mince mixture into an ovenproof dish for the older child with four slices of potato overlapping over the top, then add a slice of aubergine and three slices of courgette.

8 Stir the spices, garlic and seasoning into the remaining lamb mixture, and cook for 1 minute and then spoon into a 1.2 litre/ 2 pint/5 cup shallow ovenproof dish discarding the bay leaf.

9 Arrange the remaining potatoes overlapping on top of the lamb, and then add the aubergine slices, tucking the courgette slices in between the aubergines in a random pattern.

10 To make the sauce, melt the margarine in a small saucepan, stir in the flour then gradually add the milk and bring to the boil, stirring until thickened and smooth. Add a pinch of nutmeg and a little salt and pepper.

11 Pour a little of the sauce over the toddler's portion then pour the rest over the adults' portion. Sprinkle the larger dish with Parmesan cheese and 15ml/3 tsp breadcrumbs, sprinkling the remaining breadcrumbs over the toddler's portion.

12 Cook the moussakas in the oven. The larger dish will take 45 minutes while the toddler's portion will take about 25 minutes. Reheat the baby portion, and test the temperature of the children's food before serving.

1 Dry fry the onion and minced lamb in a saucepan until browned, stirring. Add the tomatoes and bay leaf, bring to the boil, stirring, then cover and simmer for 30 minutes.

2 Place the aubergine slices in a single layer on a baking sheet, sprinkle with a little salt and set aside for 20 minutes. Preheat oven to 200°C/400°F/Gas 6.

Chilli con Carne

3 medium baking potatoes
1 onion, chopped
450g/1lb lean minced beef
1 carrot, chopped
½ red pepper, cored, seeded and diced
400g/14oz can tomatoes
10ml/2 tsp tomato purée
150ml/¼ pint/⅔ cup beef stock
3 small bay leaves
30ml/2 tbsp olive oil
115g/4oz button mushrooms, sliced
2 garlic cloves, crushed
10ml/2 tsp mild chilli powder
2.5ml/½ tsp ground cumin
5ml/1 tsp ground coriander
200g/7oz can red kidney beans, drained
40g/1½oz frozen mixed vegetables
15ml/1 tbsp milk
knob of butter or margarine
60ml/4 tbsp fromage frais or Greek yogurt
15ml/1 tbsp chopped fresh coriander leaves
salt and freshly ground black pepper
green salad, to serve

1 Preheat the oven to 180°C/ 350°F/Gas 4. Scrub and prick the potatoes and cook in the oven for 1½ hours. Dry fry the onion and minced beef in a saucepan until browned. Add the carrot and red pepper and cook for 2 minutes.

2 Add the tomatoes, tomato purée and stock and bring to the boil. Transfer one quarter of the mixture to a 600ml/1 pint/2½ cup casserole dish, add 1 of the bay leaves, cover with a lid and set aside.

3 Spoon the remaining mince mixture into a 1.2 litre/2 pint/ 5 cup casserole. Heat 15ml/1 tbsp of the oil in the same pan and fry the mushrooms and garlic for 3 minutes.

4 Stir in the spices and seasoning, cook for 1 minute then add the drained red kidney beans and the remaining bay leaves and stir into the meat mixture. Cover and cook both dishes in the oven for 1 hour.

5 When the potatoes are cooked, cut into halves or quarters and scoop out the potato leaving a thin layer of potato on the skin.

6 Brush the potato skins with the remaining oil and grill for 10 minutes until browned.

7 Boil the frozen mixed vegetables for 5 minutes and mash the potato centres with milk and a knob of butter or margarine.

8 Spoon the mince from the smaller casserole into an ovenproof ramekin dish for the toddler and the rest into a bowl for baby. Top both with some of the mashed potato.

9 Drain the vegetables, arrange two pea eyes, carrot pieces for the mouth and mixed vegetables for hair on the toddler's dish.

10 Spoon the remaining vegetables into a baby bowl and chop or process to the desired consistency. Test the temperature of the children's food before serving.

11 Spoon the adults' chilli on to warmed serving plates, add the potato skins and top with fromage frais and chopped coriander. Serve with a green salad.

Beef Bourguignon with Creamed Potatoes

450g/1lb stewing beef

15ml/1 tbsp sunflower oil

1 onion, chopped

30ml/2 tbsp plain flour

300ml/½ pint/1¼ cups beef stock

15ml/1 tbsp tomato purée

small bunch of fresh herbs or 1.5ml/ ¼ tsp dried

2 garlic cloves, crushed

90ml/6 tbsp red wine

75g/3oz shallots

75g/3oz button mushrooms

25g/1oz/2 tbsp butter

450g/1lb potatoes

175g/6oz green cabbage

30–60ml/2–4 tbsp milk

salt and freshly ground black pepper

a few fresh herbs, to garnish

1 Preheat the oven to 160°C/ 325°F/Gas 3. Trim away any fat from the beef and cut into cubes.

2 Heat the oil in a frying pan, add half of the beef and fry until browned. Transfer to a plate and fry the remaining beef and the chopped onion until browned.

3 Return the first batch of beef to the pan with any meat juices, stir in the flour and then add the stock and tomato purée. Bring to the boil, stirring, until thickened.

4 Spoon one-third of the beef mixture into a small 600ml/ ½ pint/1¼ cup casserole dish for the children, making sure that the meat is well covered with stock. Add a few fresh herbs or half a dried bay leaf. Set the casserole aside.

5 Add the remaining herbs, garlic, wine and seasoning to the beef in the frying pan and bring to the boil. Transfer the beef to a 1.2 litre/2 pint/5 cup casserole dish. Cover both dishes and cook in the oven for 2 hours or until the meat is very tender.

6 Meanwhile, halve the shallots if large, wipe and slice the mushrooms, cover and put to one side.

7 Half an hour before the end of cooking, fry the shallots in a little butter until browned, then add the mushrooms and fry for 2–3 minutes. Stir into the larger casserole and cook for the remaining time.

8 Cut the potatoes into chunky pieces and cook in a saucepan of boiling, salted water for 20 minutes. Shred the cabbage, discarding the hard core, rinse and steam above the potatoes for the last 5 minutes.

9 Drain the potatoes and mash with 30ml/2 tbsp of the milk and the remaining butter.

10 Chop or process one-third of the child's casserole with a spoonful of cabbage, adding extra milk if necessary. Spoon into a dish for the baby, with a little potato.

11 Spoon the remaining child's casserole on to a plate for the toddler. Remove any bay leaf and cut up any large pieces of beef. Add potato and cabbage.

12 Garnish the adults' casserole with fresh herbs and serve with potatoes and cabbage. Test the temperature of the children's food.

Osso Bucco Pork with Rice

3 pork spare rib chops, about 500g/
    1¼lb

15ml/1 tbsp olive oil

1 onion, chopped

1 large carrot, chopped

2 celery sticks, thinly sliced

2 garlic cloves, crushed

400g/14oz can tomatoes

few sprigs fresh thyme or 1.5ml/
    ¼ tsp dried

grated rind and juice of ½ lemon

150g/5oz/⅔ cup long grain rice

pinch of turmeric

115g/4oz green beans

knob of butter

20ml/4 tbsp freshly grated Parmesan
    cheese

salt and freshly ground black pepper

1 or 2 sprigs parsley

1 Preheat the oven to 180°C/
350°F/Gas 4. Rinse the chops
under cold water and pat dry.

2 Heat the oil in a large frying pan,
add the pork, brown on both
sides and transfer to a casserole dish.

3 Add the onion, carrot and celery
to the frying pan and fry for 3
minutes until lightly browned.

4 Add half the garlic, the
tomatoes, thyme and lemon
juice and bring to the boil, stirring.
Pour the mixture over the pork,
cover and cook in the oven for 1½
hours or until tender.

5 Half fill two small saucepans
with water and bring to the boil.
Add 115g/4oz/½ cup rice to one
with a pinch of turmeric and salt,
add the remaining rice to the second
pan. Return to the boil, and simmer.

6 Trim the beans and steam above
the larger pan of rice for 8
minutes or until the rice is tender.

7 Drain both pans of rice, and
return the yellow rice to the pan
and add the butter, Parmesan cheese
and a little pepper. Mix together
well and keep warm.

8 Dice one chop, discarding any
bone if necessary. Spoon a little
of the white rice on to a plate for the
toddler and add half of the diced
chop. Add a few vegetables and a
spoonful of the sauce. Process the
other half of chop, some vegetables,
rice and sauce to the desired
consistency and turn into a small
bowl for the baby.

9 Spoon the yellow rice on to the
adults' plates and add a pork
chop to each. Season the sauce to
taste and then spoon the sauce and
vegetables over the meat, discarding
the thyme sprigs if used. Finely chop
the parsley and sprinkle over the
pork with the lemon rind and the
remaining crushed garlic.

10 Serve the adult's and
toddler's portions with green
beans. Test the temperature of the
children's food before serving.

Pork Stir Fry

250g/9oz pork fillet

1 courgette

1 carrot

½ green pepper

½ red pepper

½ yellow pepper

200g/7oz packet fresh beansprouts

20ml/4 tsp sunflower oil

25g/1oz cashew nuts

150ml/¼ pint/⅔ cup chicken stock

30ml/2 tbsp tomato ketchup

10ml/2 tsp cornflour, blended with
    15ml/1 tbsp cold water

1 garlic clove, crushed

10ml/2 tsp soy sauce

20ml/4 tsp yellow bean paste or
    Hoi-Sin sauce

1 Rinse the pork under cold water, cut away any fat and thinly slice. Halve the courgette lengthways and then slice thinly, thinly slice the carrot, and cut the peppers into thin strips, discarding the core and the seeds. Place the beansprouts in a sieve and rinse well.

2 Heat 15ml/3 tsp of the oil in a wok or large frying pan, add the cashews and fry for 2 minutes until browned. Drain and reserve.

3 Add the sliced pork and stir fry for 5 minutes until browned all over and cooked through. Drain and keep warm.

4 Add the remaining oil and stir fry the courgette and carrot for 2 minutes. Add the peppers and fry for a further 2 minutes.

5 Stir in the beansprouts, stock, ketchup and the cornflour mixture, bring to the boil, stirring until the sauce has thickened.

6 Transfer 1 large spoonful of the vegetables to a bowl and 2–3 large spoonfuls to a plate for the children and set aside. Add the garlic and soy sauce to the pan and cook for 1 minute.

7 Chop or process four slices of pork with the baby's reserved vegetables to the desired consistency and turn into a baby bowl. Arrange six slices of pork on the child's plate with the reserved vegetables. Spoon the vegetables in the wok on to two adult serving plates.

8 Return the remaining pork to the wok with the nuts and yellow bean paste or Hoi-Sin sauce and cook for 1 minute, spoon on to the adults' plates and serve immediately. Test the temperature of the children's food before serving.

Sausage Casserole

450g/1lb large sausages

15ml/1 tbsp sunflower oil

1 onion, chopped

225g/8oz carrots, chopped

400g/14oz can mixed beans in water, drained

15ml/1 tbsp plain flour

450ml/¾ pint/1⅞ cup beef stock

15ml/1 tbsp Worcestershire sauce

15ml/3 tsp tomato purée

15ml/3 tsp soft brown sugar

10ml/2 tsp Dijon mustard

1 bay leaf

1 dried chilli, chopped

3 medium baking potatoes

salt and freshly ground black pepper

butter and sprigs of fresh parsley, to serve

1 Preheat the oven to 180°C/ 350°F/Gas 4. Prick and separate the sausages.

2 Heat the oil in a frying pan, add the sausages and cook over a high heat until evenly browned but not cooked through. Drain and transfer to a plate.

3 Add the chopped onion and carrots to the pan and fry until lightly browned. Add the drained beans and flour, stir well and then spoon one-third of the mixture into a small casserole. Stir in 150ml/ ¼ pint/⅔ cup stock, 5ml/1 tsp tomato purée and 5ml/1 tsp sugar.

4 Add the Worcestershire sauce, remaining beef stock, tomato purée and sugar to the pan, together with the mustard, bay leaf and chopped chilli. Season and bring to the boil, then pour the mixture into a large casserole.

5 Add two sausages to the small casserole and the rest to the larger dish. Cover both and cook in the oven for 1½ hours.

6 Scrub and prick the potatoes and cook on a shelf above the casserole for 1½ hours until tender.

7 Spoon two-thirds of the child's casserole on to a plate for the toddler. Slice the sausages and give him or her two-thirds. Halve one of the baked potatoes, add a knob of butter and place on the toddler's plate.

8 Scoop the potato from the other half and mash or process with the remaining child's beans to the desired consistency for baby. Spoon into a dish and serve the remaining sausage slices as finger food.

9 Spoon the adults' casserole on to plates, halve the other potatoes, add butter and garnish with parsley. Test the temperature of the children's food.

PERFECT POULTRY

WHATEVER THE AGE OF THE DINER, CHICKEN AND TURKEY ARE ALWAYS POPULAR. AVAILABLE IN A RANGE OF CUTS AND PRICES THERE'S SOMETHING TO SUIT ALL BUDGETS AND TASTES FROM A TASTY SALAD TO PAN FRIED TURKEY, TANDOORI STYLE MARINADE OR STUFFED CHICKEN BREASTS WITH PESTO, HAM AND CHEESE.

Chicken and Thyme Casserole

6 chicken thighs

15ml/1 tbsp olive oil

1 onion, chopped

30ml/2 tbsp plain flour

300ml/½ pint/1¼ cups chicken stock

few sprigs fresh thyme or 1.5 ml/ ¼ tsp dried

To Serve

350g/12oz new potatoes

1 large carrot

115g/4oz/¾ cup frozen peas

5ml/1 tsp Dijon mustard

grated rind and juice of ½ orange

60ml/4 tbsp fromage frais or natural yogurt

salt and freshly ground black pepper

fresh thyme or parsley, to garnish

1 Preheat the oven to 180°C/ 350°F/Gas 4. Rinse the chicken under cold water and pat dry.

2 Heat the oil in a large frying pan, add the chicken and brown on both sides, then transfer to a casserole.

3 Add the onion and fry, stirring until lightly browned. Stir in the flour, then add the stock and thyme and bring to the boil, stirring.

4 Pour over the chicken, cover and cook in the oven for 1 hour or until tender.

5 Meanwhile scrub the potatoes and cut any large ones in half. Cut the carrot into matchsticks.

6 Cook the potatoes in boiling water 15 minutes before the chicken is ready and cook the carrots and peas in a separate pan of boiling water for 5 minutes. Drain.

7 Take one chicken thigh out of the casserole, remove the skin and cut the meat away from the bone. Place in a baby bowl or a food processor or blender with some of the vegetables and gravy and chop or process to the desired consistency. Turn into a baby bowl.

8 Take a second chicken thigh out of the casserole for the toddler, remove the skin and bone and slice if necessary. Arrange on a plate with some of the vegetables and gravy. Test the temperature of the children's food before serving.

9 Arrange two chicken thighs on to warmed serving plates for the adults. Stir the mustard, orange rind and juice, fromage frais and seasoning into the hot sauce and then spoon over the chicken. Serve at once, with the vegetables, garnished with a sprig of thyme or parsley.

Tandoori Style Chicken

6 chicken thighs

150g/5oz natural yogurt

6.5ml/1¼ tsp paprika

5ml/1 tsp hot curry paste

5ml/1 tsp coriander seeds, roughly
crushed

2.5ml/½ tsp cumin seeds, roughly
crushed

2.5ml/½ tsp turmeric

pinch of dried mixed herbs

5ml/2 tsp sunflower oil

To Serve

350g/12oz new potatoes

3 celery sticks

10cm/4in piece cucumber

15ml/1 tbsp olive oil

5ml/1 tsp white wine vinegar

5ml/1 tsp mint jelly

salt and freshly ground black pepper

few sprigs of watercress, knob of
butter and cherry tomatoes, to
serve

1 Cut away the skin from the
chicken thighs and slash the
meat two or three times with a small
knife. Rinse under cold water and
pat dry.

2 Place four thighs in a shallow
dish, the other two on a plate.
Place the yogurt, 5ml/1 tsp of the
paprika, the curry paste, both seeds
and almost all the turmeric into a
small bowl and mix together. Spoon
over the four chicken thighs.

3 Sprinkle the remaining paprika
and the mixed herbs over the
other chicken thighs and sprinkle the
remaining pinch of turmeric over 1
thigh. Cover both dishes loosely
with clear film and chill in the
refrigerator for 2–3 hours.

4 Preheat the oven to 200°C/
400°F/Gas 6. Arrange the
chicken thighs on a roasting rack set
over a small roasting tin and drizzle
oil over the herby chicken. Pour a
little boiling water into base of the
tin and cook for 45–50 minutes or
until the juices run clear when the
chicken is pierced with a skewer.

5 Meanwhile, scrub the potatoes
and halve any large ones. Cook
in a saucepan of boiling water for 15
minutes until tender.

6 Cut one celery stick and a small
piece of cucumber into
matchsticks. Chop or shred the
remaining celery and cucumber.

7 Blend together the oil, vinegar,
mint jelly and seasoning in a
bowl and add the chopped or
shredded celery, cucumber and
watercress, tossing well to coat.

8 Drain the potatoes and toss in a
little butter. Divide the potatoes
among the adults' plates, toddler's
dish and the baby bowl. Cut the
chicken off the bone for the toddler
and arrange on a plate with half of
the celery and cucumber sticks.

9 Cut the remaining chicken thigh
into tiny pieces for the baby,
discarding the bone, and allow to
cool. Add to the bowl with the
cooled potatoes and vegetable sticks
and allow baby to feed him- or
herself. Add a few halved tomatoes
to each portion. Test the temperature
of children's food before serving.

10 For the adults, arrange the
chicken thighs on warmed
serving plates with the potatoes.
Serve with the piquant salad.

Chicken Wrappers

3 boneless, skinless chicken breasts

5ml/1 tsp pesto

40g/1½oz wafer thin ham

50g/2oz Cheddar cheese

350g/12oz new potatoes

175g/6oz green beans

15g/½oz/1 tbsp butter

10ml/2 tsp olive oil

1 tomato

6 stoned black olives

10ml/2 tsp plain flour

150ml/¼ pint/⅔ cup chicken stock

15ml/1 tbsp crème fraîche or soured
  cream (optional)

few sprigs of fresh basil (optional)

1 Rinse the chicken under cold
  water and pat dry. Put one
chicken breast between two pieces of
clear film and bat out with a rolling
pin until half as big again. Repeat
with the other two chicken breasts.

TIP
Depending on the age of the baby,
you may prefer to omit the sauce
and serve the meal as finger food,
cutting it into more manageable
pieces first.

2 Spread pesto over two of the
  chicken breasts and divide the
ham among all three. Cut the cheese
into three thick slices then add one to
each piece of chicken. Roll up so that
the cheese is completely enclosed,
then secure with string.

3 Scrub the potatoes, halve any
  large ones and cook in a
saucepan of boiling water for 15
minutes until tender. Trim the beans
and cook in a separate pan of boiling
water for 10 minutes.

4 Meanwhile, heat the butter and
  oil in a large frying pan, add the
chicken and cook for about 10
minutes, turning several times, until
well browned and cooked through.

5 Lift the chicken out of the pan,
  keeping those spread with pesto
warm, and leaving the other one to
cool slightly.

6 Cut the tomato into wedges and
  halve the olives. Stir in the flour
and cook for 1 minute. Gradually
stir in the stock and bring to the boil,
stirring until thickened. Add the
tomato and olives.

7 Snip the string off the chicken
  and slice the children's chicken
breast thinly. Arrange four chicken
slices on a child's plate with a couple
of spoonfuls of sauce and a few
potatoes and green beans. (Don't
offer olives unless the child is a very
adventurous eater.)

8 Chop or process the remaining
  cut chicken with 30ml/2 tbsp of
the sauce, one or two potatoes and
three green beans to the desired
consistency. Test the temperature of
the children's food before serving.

9 Arrange the remaining chicken
  on plates. Add the crème fraîche
or soured cream to the pan, if using,
and heat gently. Spoon over the
chicken and serve with vegetables.

Pan Fried Turkey with Coriander

3 turkey breast steaks

1 onion

1 red pepper, cored and seeded

15ml/1 tbsp sunflower oil

5ml/1 tsp plain flour

150ml/¼ pint/⅔ cup chicken stock

30ml/2 tbsp frozen sweetcorn

150g/5oz/⅔ cup long grain white rice

1 garlic clove

1 dried chilli

50g/2oz creamed coconut

30ml/2 tbsp chopped fresh coriander

fresh coriander sprigs and lime wedges, to serve

1 Rinse the turkey steaks under cold water, and pat dry. Chop one of the steaks, finely chop one quarter of the onion and dice one quarter of the red pepper. Heat 5ml/ 1 tsp of the oil in a small frying pan and fry the diced turkey and chopped onion until lightly browned all over.

2 Stir in the flour, add the stock, sweetcorn and chopped pepper, then bring to the boil, cover and simmer for 10 minutes.

3 Cook the long grain rice in boiling water for 8–10 minutes or until just tender. Drain.

4 Meanwhile process or finely chop the remaining pieces of onion and red pepper with the garlic and chilli, including the seeds if you like hot food.

5 Put the creamed coconut into a bowl, pour on 200 ml/7fl oz/ 1 cup boiling water and stir until the coconut is completely dissolved.

6 Heat the remaining oil in a large frying pan. Brown the turkey breasts on one side, turn over and add the pepper paste. Fry for 5 minutes until the second side of the turkey is also browned.

7 Pour the coconut milk over the turkey and cook for 2–3 minutes, stirring until the sauce has thickened slightly. Sprinkle with the chopped fresh coriander.

8 Chop or process one-third of the children's portion with 30ml/ 2 tbsp of the rice until the desired consistency is reached. Spoon into a baby bowl.

9 Spoon the child's portion on to a child's plate and serve with a little rice. Test the temperature of the children's food before serving.

10 Spoon the rest of the rice on to warmed serving plates for the adults, add the turkey and sauce and garnish with coriander sprigs and lime wedges.

Chicken Salad

3 chicken breasts, boned and skinned

½ onion, chopped

1 carrot, chopped

150ml/¼ pint/⅔ cup chicken stock

few fresh herbs or a pinch of dried
  mixed herbs

30ml/2 tbsp butter or sunflower
  margarine

15ml/1 tbsp plain flour

30ml/2 tbsp frozen sweetcorn,
  defrosted

3 slices bread

2 celery sticks

1 green dessert apple

1 red dessert apple

mixed green salad leaves and 1 small
  tomato, cut into wedges, to serve

For the Dressing

45ml/3 tbsp natural yogurt

45ml/3 tbsp mayonnaise

5ml/1 tsp ground coriander

salt and freshly ground black pepper

1 Rinse the chicken breasts under cold water and place in a saucepan with the chopped onion and carrot, stock and herbs. Cover and cook for 15 minutes or until the chicken is cooked through.

2 Cut one chicken breast into small dice, cutting the other two into larger pieces.

3 Strain the stock into a jug, finely chop the carrot and remove and discard the onion and herbs.

4 Preheat the oven to 190°C/ 375°F/Gas 5. Melt 15ml/1 tbsp of the butter or margarine in a small saucepan, stir in the flour and then gradually stir in the strained stock and bring to the boil, stirring until the sauce is thickened and smooth. Add the finely diced chicken, carrot and sweetcorn.

5 Cut the bread into three 7.5cm/ 3in squares, cutting the trimmings into tiny shapes using cutters. Spread both sides of the squares and one side of the tiny bread shapes with the remaining butter or margarine. Press the squares into sections of a bun tray.

6 Bake the small shapes in the oven for 5 minutes and the squares for 10 minutes, until crisp and golden brown all over.

7 Rinse and thinly slice the celery, and quarter, core and chop half of each of the apples.

8 To make the salad dressing, blend the yogurt, mayonnaise, ground coriander and salt and pepper in a bowl. Add the thickly diced chicken and the celery, pepper and apples and mix together.

9 Tear the salad leaves into pieces and arrange on the adults' serving plates. Spoon the chicken salad over the salad leaves.

10 Chop or process half of the child's chicken mixture to the desired consistency for the baby and spoon into a dish with the tiny bread shapes. Reheat the remaining mixture if necessary, spoon into the bread cases and arrange on a plate for the toddler. Slice the two apple halves, cutting the peel away from a few slices and add to the children's dishes. Check the temperature of hot food before serving to children.

FISHY DINNERS

QUICK TO MAKE FOR EVERYDAY OR A SPECIAL OCCASION – HERE ARE SOME FISH RECIPES FOR ANY DAY OF THE WEEK. CHOOSE FROM FRESH, FROZEN OR CANNED FISH FOR ADDED CONVENIENCE. FORGET ABOUT PLAIN FISHFINGERS AND ENCOURAGE THE CHILDREN TO TRY HOMEMADE FISH CAKES WITH A TASTY SAUCE FOR THE ADULTS, PAELLA, EYE-CATCHING FISHY VOL-AU-VENTS OR COLOURFUL SALMON AND COD KEBABS.

Paella

400g/14oz cod fillet

115g/4oz fish cocktail or a mixture of prawns, mussels and squid

15ml/1 tbsp olive oil

1 onion, chopped

1 garlic clove, crushed

150g/5oz/⅔ cup long grain white rice

pinch of saffron or turmeric

few sprigs of fresh thyme or pinch dried

225g/8oz can tomatoes

½ red pepper, cored, seeded and chopped

½ green pepper, cored, seeded and chopped

50g/2oz frozen peas

30ml/2 tbsp fresh chopped parsley

salt and freshly ground black pepper

1 Remove any skin from the cod and place the fish cocktail in a sieve and rinse well with cold water.

2 Heat the oil in a frying pan, add the onion and fry until lightly browned, stirring occasionally. Add the garlic and 115g/4oz/½ cup of the rice and cook for 1 minute.

3 Add the saffron or turmeric, thyme, 2 of the canned tomatoes, 350ml/12fl oz/1½ cups water and salt and pepper. Bring to the boil and cook for 5 minutes.

4 Put the remaining rice and canned tomatoes in a small saucepan with 90ml/3fl oz/⅓ cup water. Cover the pan and cook for about 5 minutes.

5 Add 15ml/1 tbsp of the mixed peppers and 15ml/1 tbsp of the frozen peas to the small pan, adding all the remaining vegetables to the large pan. Place 115g/4oz of the fish in a metal sieve, cutting in half if necessary. Place above a small pan of boiling water, cover and steam for 5 minutes. Add the remaining fish to the paella in the large pan, cover the pan and cook for 5 minutes.

6 Add the fish cocktail to the paella, cover the pan and cook for a further 3 minutes.

7 Stir the chopped parsley into the paella and spoon on to two warmed serving plates for the adults. Spoon half of the tomato rice mixture and half the fish on to a plate for the child and process the remaining fish and rice to the desired consistency for baby. Spoon into a dish and check both children's meals for bones. Test the temperature of the children's food before serving.

Fish Cakes

450g/1lb potatoes, cut into pieces
450g/1lb cod fillet
75g/3oz prepared spinach leaves
75ml/5 tbsp full-fat milk
25g/1oz/2 tbsp butter
1 egg
50g/2oz/1 cup fresh breadcrumbs
25g/1oz drained sun-dried tomatoes
25g/1oz drained stuffed olives
115g/4oz Greek yogurt
3 tomatoes, cut into wedges
½ small onion, thinly sliced
15ml/1 tbsp frozen peas, cooked
sunflower oil, for frying
salt and pepper
lemon wedges and green salad, to serve

3 Peel away the skin from the fish, and break into small flakes, carefully removing any bones. Chop the spinach and add to the potato with the fish.

4 For baby, spoon 45ml/3 tbsp of the mixture into a bowl and mash with another 30ml/2 tbsp milk. Add a little salt and pepper, if liked, to the remaining fish mixture.

5 For the older child, shape three tablespoons of mixture into three small rounds with floured hands. For adults, shape the remaining mixture into four cakes.

1 Half fill a large saucepan or steamer base with water, add the potatoes and bring to the boil. Place the cod in a steamer top or in a colander above the saucepan. Cover and cook for 8–10 minutes or until the fish flakes easily when pressed.

2 Take the fish out of the steamer and place on a plate. Add the spinach to the steamer, cook for 3 minutes until just wilted and transfer to a dish. Test the potatoes, cook for 1–2 minutes more if necessary, then drain and mash with 30ml/2 tbsp of the milk and the butter.

TIP
Make sure you remove all bones from the fish.

6 Beat the egg and the remaining milk on a plate. Place the breadcrumbs on a second plate and dip both the toddler and the adult fish cakes first into the egg and then into the crumb mixture.

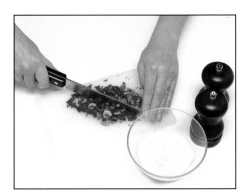

7 Chop the sun-dried tomatoes and stuffed olives and stir into the yogurt with a little salt and pepper. Spoon into a small dish.

8 Heat some oil in a frying pan and fry the small cakes for 2–3 minutes each side until browned. Drain well and arrange on a child's plate. Add tomato wedges for tails, peas for eyes.

9 Fry the adult fish cakes in more oil if necessary for 3–4 minutes each side until browned and heated through. Drain and serve with the dip, lemon and tomato wedges, thinly sliced onion and a green salad. Reheat the baby portion if necessary but test the temperature of the children's food before serving.

Fishy Vol-au-Vents

250g/9oz puff pastry, thawed if frozen

a little flour

beaten egg, to glaze

350g/12oz cod fillet

200ml/7fl oz/⅓ cup milk

½ leek

30ml/2 tbsp sunflower margarine

30ml/2 tbsp plain flour

50g/2oz fresh prawns

salt and pepper

broccoli, young carrots and mange tout, to serve

1 Preheat the oven to 220°C/ 425°F/Gas 7. Roll out the pastry on a lightly floured surface to make a rectangle 23 × 15cm/9 × 6in. Cut into three 7cm/3in wide strips.

2 Cut two fish shapes from one strip. Knock up edges with a knife and cut an oval shape just in from the edge and almost through to the bottom of the pastry. Place the fish shape on a wetted baking tray.

TIP
You may find it easier to cut a fish shape out of paper and then use this as a template on the pastry.

3 Neaten the edges of the remaining pastry strips then cut smaller rectangles 1cm/½in in from the edge of both and remove.

4 Roll out the smaller rectangles to the same size as the pastry frames. Brush the edges with a little egg and place the frames on top.

5 Transfer to the baking sheet. Knock up the edges of both rectangles with a small knife and flute between finger and thumb. Repeat the whole process with the third strip of pastry.

6 Stamp out tiny fish shapes from the pastry trimmings, rerolling if necessary, and place on the baking sheet. Brush the top of the vol-au-vents with beaten egg and cook for 10 minutes, remove the small fish and cook the larger vol-au-vents for a further 5 minutes until they are well risen and golden brown.

7 Meanwhile make the filling. Cut the fish in two and put in a saucepan with the milk. Halve the leek lengthways, wash thoroughly then slice and add to the pan.

8 Cover and simmer for 6–8 minutes or until the fish flakes easily when pressed with a knife. Lift out of the pan, peel away the skin and then break into pieces, removing and discarding any bones.

9 Strain the milk, reserving the leeks. Melt the margarine, stir in the flour and then gradually add in the milk and bring to the boil, stirring until thick and smooth.

10 Stir the fish into the sauce. Scoop out the centres of the fish-shaped vol-au-vents and fill with a little mixture. Spoon 30ml/2 tbsp of fish mixture into a baby bowl.

11 Add a prawn to each fish-shaped vol-au-vent and stir the rest into the saucepan with the leeks and a little seasoning. Heat gently and spoon into the two large pastry cases. Transfer to plates and serve with steamed vegetables.

12 Chop the baby portion with some vegetables and serve this with some tiny pastry fishes, if wished, in a small bowl. Check the temperature of the children's food before serving.

Salmon and Cod Kebabs

200g/7oz salmon steak

275g/10oz cod fillet

15ml/3 tsp lemon juice

10ml/2 tsp olive oil

2.5ml/½ tsp Dijon mustard

salt and freshly ground black pepper

350g/12oz new potatoes

200g/7oz frozen peas

50g/2oz/4 tbsp butter

15–30ml/1–2 tbsp milk

3 tomatoes, chopped, seeds
   discarded

¼ round lettuce, finely shredded

For the Mustard Sauce

1 sprig fresh dill

20ml/4 tsp mayonnaise

5ml/1 tsp Dijon mustard

5ml/1 tsp lemon juice

2.5ml/½ tsp dark brown sugar

2 Cut a few pieces of fish into smaller pieces and thread on to five cocktail sticks. Thread the remaining fish pieces on to long wooden skewers.

3 Mix together the lemon juice, oil, Dijon mustard and a little salt and pepper to taste in a small bowl and set aside.

4 Finely chop the dill and place in a bowl with the other sauce ingredients and mix. Set aside.

5 Scrub the potatoes, halve any large ones and then cook in lightly salted water for 15 minutes or until tender. Place the peas and half of the butter in a frying pan, cover and cook very gently for 5 minutes.

1 Rinse the fish under cold water and pat dry. Cut the salmon steak in half, cutting around the central bone. Cut away the skin and then cut into chunky cubes making sure you remove any bones. Remove the skin from the cod and cut into similar sized pieces.

6 Preheat the grill, place the kebabs on a baking sheet and brush the larger kebabs with the lemon, oil and mustard mixture. Grill for 5 minutes, until the fish is cooked, turning once.

7 Remove the fish from two cocktail sticks and mix in a small bowl with a few new potatoes and 15ml/1 tbsp of the peas. Chop or process with a little milk until the desired consistency is reached, then transfer to a baby bowl.

8 Arrange the toddler's kebabs on a small serving plate with a few potatoes, 30ml/2 tbsp peas and a small amount of chopped tomato. Test the temperature of the children's food before serving.

9 Add the tomatoes to the remaining peas and cook for 2 minutes, stir in the shredded lettuce and cook for 1 minute. Spoon on to serving plates for the adults, add the kebabs and potatoes and serve.

TIP
Depending on the age of the toddler, you may prefer to remove the cocktail sticks before serving.

Tuna Florentine

50g/2oz pasta shapes

175g/6oz fresh spinach leaves

50g/2oz frozen mixed vegetables

200g/7oz can tuna fish in brine

2 eggs

buttered toast and grilled tomatoes,
  to serve

For the Sauce

25g/1oz/2 tbsp sunflower margarine

45ml/3 tbsp plain flour

300ml/½ pint/1¼ cups milk

50g/2 oz/½ cup grated Cheddar
  cheese

1 Cook the pasta in boiling water
for 10 minutes. Meanwhile tear
off any spinach stalks, wash the
leaves in plenty of cold water and
place in a steamer or colander.

2 Stir the frozen vegetables into
the pasta as it is cooking, and
then place the spinach in the steamer
over the top. Cover and cook for the
last 3 minutes or until the spinach
has just wilted.

TIP
Frozen vegetables are usually
more nutritious than fresh
vegetables as they are frozen at
their peak of perfection – they're
a great time saver too.

3 Drain the pasta and vegetables
through a sieve. Chop one
quarter of the spinach and add to the
pasta and vegetables, dividing the
remainder between two shallow
300ml/½ pint/1¼ cup ovenproof
dishes for the adults.

4 Drain the tuna and divide
among the dishes and sieve.

5 Refill the pasta pan with water,
bring to the boil then break the
eggs into the water and gently
simmer until the egg whites are set.
Remove the eggs with a slotted
spoon, trim the whites and shake off
all the water. Arrange the eggs on
top of the tuna for the adults.

6 To make the sauce, melt the
margarine in a small saucepan,
stir in the flour, then gradually add
the milk and bring to the boil,
stirring until thickened and smooth.

7 Stir the cheese into the sauce,
reserving a little for the topping.
Spoon the sauce over the adults'
portions until the eggs are covered.
Stir the children's pasta, vegetables
and tuna into the remaining sauce
and mix together.

8 Spoon the pasta on to a plate for
the toddler and chop or process
the remainder for baby, adding a
little extra milk if necessary to make
the desired consistency. Spoon into a
dish. Test the temperature of the
children's food before serving.

9 Preheat the grill, sprinkle the
adults' portions with the
reserved cheese and grill for 4–5
minutes until browned. Serve with
buttered toast and grilled tomatoes.

VEGETABLE FEASTS

MORE AND MORE OF US ARE OPTING TO EAT LESS MEAT FOR EITHER HEALTH OR BUDGET REASONS. EATING LESS MEAT DOESN'T MEAN LOSING OUT ON FLAVOUR: FAR FROM IT! CHOOSE FROM MEALS SUCH AS CHEESE ON TOAST, CHEESY VEGETABLE CRUMBLE OR SLOW-COOKED SPICED VEGETABLE TAGINE.

Cheese on Toast

2 slices thick bread

2 slices thin bread

butter or sunflower margarine, for spreading

5ml/1 tsp Marmite

2 slices wafer thin ham

1 garlic clove, halved

15ml/1 tbsp olive oil

200g/7oz Cheddar cheese

1 tomato

6 stoned black olives

15ml/1 tbsp chopped fresh basil

a few red onion slices

cucumber sticks and green salad, to serve (optional)

2 Drizzle the oil over the thick slices of toast then rub with the cut surface of the garlic.

4 Slice the tomato and halve the olives. Arrange on the thick toast for the adults, season with pepper and add basil and onion.

3 Thinly slice the cheese and place over all of the pieces of toast.

1 Toast all the bread and spread the thin slices with butter or margarine. Spread one slice with Marmite and top this with ham.

5 Grill until the cheese is bubbly. Cut the plain cheese on toast into tiny squares, discarding crusts. Arrange on a small plate for baby and allow to cool. Cut the Marmite and cheese toast into triangles and arrange on a plate. Add cucumber sticks to the toddler's portion and test the temperature before serving.

6 Slice the adults' toast and arrange on plates with a green salad if liked, and serve.

Penne with Tomato Sauce

150g/5oz penne or small pasta quills

1 onion

2 celery sticks

1 red pepper

15ml/1 tbsp olive oil

1 garlic clove, crushed

400g/14oz can tomatoes

2.5ml/½ tsp caster sugar

8 stoned black olives

10ml/2 tsp pesto

1.5ml/¼ tsp dried chilli seeds (optional)

50g/2oz/½ cup grated Cheddar cheese

salt and freshly ground black pepper

10ml/2 tsp freshly grated Parmesan cheese, to serve

green salad, to serve (optional)

2 Meanwhile chop the onion and the celery. Cut the pepper in half, then scoop out the core and seeds and dice the pepper finely.

3 Heat the oil in a second saucepan, add the vegetables and garlic and fry for 5 minutes, stirring until lightly browned.

1 Cook the pasta in salted boiling water for about 10–12 minutes until just tender.

4 Add the tomatoes and sugar and cook for 5 minutes, stirring occasionally until the tomatoes are broken up and pulpy.

5 Drain the pasta, return to the pan and stir in the tomato sauce.

6 Spoon 45–60ml/3–4 tbsp of the mixture into a bowl or processor and chop or process to the desired consistency for baby. Spoon 75–90ml/5–6 tbsp of the mixture into a bowl for the toddler.

7 Quarter the olives and stir into the remaining pasta with the pesto, chilli seeds if using, and a little salt and pepper. Spoon into dishes.

8 Sprinkle the grated Cheddar cheese over all the dishes, and serve the adults' portions with the Parmesan cheese and a green salad, if wished. Test the temperature of the children's food before serving.

Courgette Gougère

50g/2oz/4 tbsp butter

65g/2½oz plain flour

2 eggs

2.5ml/½ tsp Dijon mustard

115g/4oz Cheddar cheese

salt and pepper

For the Filling

15ml/1 tbsp olive oil

350g/12oz courgettes, sliced

1 small onion, chopped

115g/4oz button mushrooms, sliced

225g/8oz tomatoes, skinned and chopped

1 garlic clove, crushed

20ml/4 tsp chopped fresh basil

1 Preheat the oven to 220°C/ 425°F/Gas 7 and grease a large baking sheet. Place the butter in a medium-sized saucepan with 150ml/ ¼ pint/⅔ cup water. Heat gently until the butter has melted then bring to the boil.

2 Remove the pan from the heat and quickly add the flour, stir well then return to the heat and cook for 1–2 minutes, stirring constantly until the mixture forms a smooth ball. Leave to cool for 10 minutes.

3 Beat the eggs, mustard and a little salt and pepper together. Cut 25g/1oz of the cheese into small cubes and grate the rest.

4 Add 50g/2oz of the grated cheese to the dough and then gradually beat in the eggs to make a smooth, glossy paste.

5 Spoon the mixture into a large piping bag fitted with a medium plain tube. Pipe whirls close together on the baking sheet to make an 18cm/7in circular shape.

6 Pipe the remaining mixture into small balls for baby and into the older child's initials.

7 Sprinkle the top with the remaining grated cheese.

8 Bake for 15–18 minutes for the small shapes and 25 for the ring, until well risen and browned.

9 Heat the oil in a frying pan, add the courgettes and onion and fry until lightly browned. Add the mushrooms, fry for a further 2 minutes and then add the tomatoes. Cover and simmer for 5 minutes until the vegetables are cooked.

10 Spoon a little mixture into baby's bowl or into a processor and chop or process to the desired consistency. Serve with a few cheesy balls and a little diced cheese.

11 Spoon a little on to a plate for the toddler, add a cheesy initial and the remaining diced cheese. Test the temperature of the children's food before serving.

12 Transfer the cheesy ring to a serving plate and split in half horizontally. Stir the garlic, basil and a little extra seasoning into the courgette mixture and heat through. Spoon over the bottom half of the cheese ring and add top half. Serve the gougère immediately.

TIP
Beat the gougère mixture, cheese and eggs together in a food processor if preferred.

Cheesy Vegetable Crumble

1 onion

225g/8oz carrot

175g/6oz swede

175g/6oz parsnip

15ml/1 tbsp olive oil

220g/7½oz can red kidney beans

10ml/2 tsp paprika

5ml/1 tsp ground cumin

15ml/1 tbsp plain flour

300ml/½ pint/1¼ cups vegetable
   stock

225g/8oz broccoli, to serve

For the Topping

115g/4oz Cheddar cheese

50g/2oz wholemeal flour

50g/2oz plain flour

50g/2oz sunflower margarine

30ml/2 tbsp sesame seeds

25g/1oz blanched almonds

salt and freshly ground black pepper

1 Preheat the oven to 190°C/
375°F/Gas 5. Peel and roughly
chop the onion and peel and cut the
carrot, swede and parsnip into small
cubes. Heat the oil in a large pan and
fry the vegetables for 5 minutes,
stirring until lightly browned.

2 Drain the kidney beans and add
to the pan with the spices and
flour. Stir well, add the stock, then
cover and simmer for 10 minutes.

3 Meanwhile make the topping.
Cut a few squares of cheese for
the baby and grate the rest. Put the
two flours in a bowl, add the
margarine and rub in with your
fingertips until the mixture
resembles fine breadcrumbs. Stir in
the grated cheese and sesame seeds.

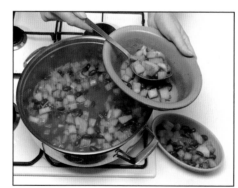

4 Spoon a little of the vegetable
mixture into a 300ml/½ pint/
1¼ cup ovenproof dish for the
toddler. Spoon the remaining
mixture into a 900ml/1½ pint/
3¾ cup ovenproof pie dish for the
adults, leaving a little vegetable
mixture in the pan for the baby.
Season the adults' portion with a
little salt and pepper.

VARIATION
Lentil and Herb Crumble
Substitute canned lentils for the red
kidney beans. Instead of the paprika
and cumin, use 2 tbsp chopped, fresh
mixed herbs. Add more fibre and
nuttiness by replacing the plain flour
with rolled oats.

5 Spoon 45ml/3 tbsp of crumble
over the older child's portion.
Roughly chop the almonds, add to
the remaining crumble with a little
salt and pepper and spoon over the
large dish. Bake in the oven for 20
minutes for the small dish, 30
minutes for the large dish, until
golden brown on top.

6 Add 90ml/3fl oz/⅓ cup water to
baby's portion, cover and cook
for 10 minutes, stirring occasionally,
until the vegetables are very tender.
Mash or process to the desired
consistency and spoon into a bowl.

7 Cut the broccoli into florets and
cook for 5 minutes or until
tender; drain. Spoon the toddler's
portion out of the dish and on to a
small plate. Serve the broccoli to all
members of the family, allowing
baby to pick up and eat the broccoli
and cubed cheese as finger food.
Check the temperature of foods
before serving to the children.

Note: Never give whole nuts to
children under 5 as they may choke.

Vegetable Tagine

1 onion
225g/8oz carrots
225g/8oz swede
75g/3oz prunes
20ml/4 tsp olive oil
425g/15oz can chick-peas
2.5ml/½ tsp turmeric
10ml/2 tsp plain flour, plus extra for dusting
2 garlic cloves, finely chopped
450ml/¾ pint/1⅞ cups chicken stock
15ml/1 tbsp tomato purée
2cm/¾in piece fresh root ginger
2.5ml/½ tsp ground cinnamon
3 cloves
115g/4oz couscous
8 green beans
2 frozen peas
piece of tomato
knob of butter or sunflower margarine
salt and freshly ground black pepper
sprig fresh coriander, to garnish

1 Peel and chop the onion and peel and dice the carrots and swede. Cut the prunes into chunky pieces, discarding the stones.

2 Heat 15ml/3 tsp of the olive oil in a large saucepan, add the onion and fry until lightly browned. Stir in the carrots and swede and fry for 3 minutes, stirring.

3 Drain the chick-peas and stir into the pan with the turmeric, flour and garlic. Add 300ml/½ pint/1¼ cup of the stock, the tomato purée, and the prunes. Bring to the boil, cover and simmer for 20 minutes, stirring occasionally.

4 Place three heaped spoonfuls of mixture in a bowl or food processor, draining off most of the liquid. Mash or process and then form the mixture into a burger with floured hands.

5 Chop or process two heaped spoonfuls of mixture and sauce to the desired consistency for baby and spoon into a bowl.

6 Finely chop the root ginger and stir into the remaining vegetable mixture with the cinnamon, cloves, remaining stock and seasoning.

7 Place the couscous in a sieve, rinse with boiling water and fluff up the grains with a fork. Place the sieve above the vegetables, cover and steam for 5 minutes.

8 Fry the veggie burger in the remaining oil until browned on both sides. Trim and cook the beans and peas for 5 minutes. Drain and arrange on a plate like an octopus with a piece of tomato for a mouth and peas for eyes.

9 Stir the butter or margarine into the couscous and fluff up the grains with a fork. Spoon on to warmed serving plates for adults, add the vegetable mixture and garnish with a sprig of coriander. Check the temperature of the children's food before serving.

Stilton and Leek Tart

175g/6oz/1½ cups plain flour

75g/3oz/6 tbsp butter

1 carrot

2 slices ham

10cm/4in piece of cucumber

mixed green salad leaves, to serve

For the Filling

25g/1oz/2 tbsp butter

115g/4oz trimmed leek, thinly sliced

75g/3oz Stilton cheese, diced

40g/1½oz Cheddar cheese, grated

3 eggs

175ml/6fl oz/¾ cup milk

pinch of paprika

salt and pepper

1 Put the flour in a bowl with a pinch of salt. Cut the butter into pieces and rub into the flour with your fingertips until the mixture resembles fine breadcrumbs.

2 Mix to a smooth dough with 30–35ml/6–7 tsp water, knead lightly and roll out thinly on a floured surface. Use to line an 18cm/7in flan dish, trimming round the edge and reserving the trimmings.

3 Reroll the trimmings and then cut out six 7.5cm/3in circles using a fluted biscuit cutter. Press the pastry circles into sections of a bun tray and chill all of the tarts.

4 Preheat the oven to 190°C/375°F/Gas 5. For the filling melt the butter in a small frying pan and fry the leek for 4–5 minutes, until soft but not brown, stirring frequently. Turn into a bowl, stir in the diced Stilton, and then spread over the base of the large tart.

5 Beat the eggs and milk together in a small bowl and season with salt and pepper.

6 Divide the grated Cheddar among the small tartlet shells and pour some of the egg mixture over. Pour the remaining egg mixture over the leek and Stilton tart and sprinkle with paprika.

7 Cook the small tartlets for 15 minutes and the large tart for 30–35 minutes until well risen and browned. Leave to cool.

8 Peel and coarsely grate the carrot. Cut the ham into triangles for "sails". Cut the ham trimmings into small strips for the baby. Cut the cucumber into batons.

9 Place a spoonful of carrot, some cucumber, a small tart and some ham trimmings in the baby dish. Spread the remaining carrot onto a plate for the older child, place the tarts on top and secure the ham "sails" with cocktail sticks. Serve any remaining tarts next day. Cut the large tart into wedges and serve with a mixed leaf salad.

JUST DESSERTS

No one can resist a dessert, although looking after a young family may mean it's more of a weekend treat than an everyday occurrence. Spoil the family with a selection of these tasty hot and cold puds from fruity Eve's Pudding and Plum Crumble to Chocolate Trifle or Orange and Strawberry Shortcakes – all guaranteed to get them clamouring for seconds.

Bread and Butter Pudding

3 dried apricots

45ml/3 tbsp sultanas

30ml/2 tbsp sherry

7 slices white bread, crusts removed

25g/1oz/½ tbsp butter, softened

30ml/2 tbsp caster sugar

pinch of ground cinnamon

4 eggs

300ml/½ pint/1¼ cups milk

few drops of vanilla essence

pinch of cinnamon

pouring cream, to serve

2 Preheat the oven to 190°C/ 375°F/Gas 5. Spread the bread with butter and cut one slice into very small triangles. Layer in a 150ml/¼ pint/⅔ cup pie dish with plain apricots and sultanas and 5ml/1 tsp of the sugar.

4 Beat the eggs, milk and vanilla together and pour into the ramekin and two pie dishes.

1 Chop two dried apricots and place in a small bowl with 30ml/ 2 tbsp of the sultanas and the sherry. Set aside for about 2 hours. Chop the remaining apricot and mix with the remaining sultanas.

3 Cut the remaining bread into larger triangles and layer in a 900ml/1½ pint/3¾ cup pie dish with the sherried fruits and all but 5ml/ 1 tsp of the remaining sugar, sprinkling the top with cinnamon. Put the last 5ml/1 tsp sugar in a small ramekin dish.

5 Stand the ramekin dish in a large ovenproof dish and half fill with hot water. Cook the small pie dish and the ramekin for 25–30 minutes until the custard is just set, the larger pudding for 35 minutes until the bread is browned. Serve the adult portions with cream, if liked.

Eve's Pudding

500g/1¼lb cooking apples

50g/2oz/¼ cup caster sugar

50g/2oz frozen or canned
  blackberries

For the Topping

50g/2oz/4 tbsp butter or sunflower
  margarine

50g/2oz/¼ cup caster sugar

50g/2oz/⅓ cup self-raising flour

1 egg

½ lemon, rind only

15ml/1 tbsp lemon juice

icing sugar, for dusting

custard, to serve

1 Preheat the oven to 180°C/
350°F/Gas 4. Peel and slice the
cooking apples, discarding core, and
then place in a saucepan with the
caster sugar and 15ml/1 tbsp water.
Cover and cook gently for 5 minutes
until the apple slices are almost
tender but still whole.

2 Half fill a 150ml/¼ pint/⅔ cup
ovenproof ramekin with apple
for the toddler and mash 30ml/2 tbsp
apple for baby in a small bowl.

3 Put the remaining apple slices in
to a 600ml/1 pint/2½ cup
ovenproof dish. Sprinkle the
blackberries over the apple slices.

4 To make the topping, place the
butter or margarine, sugar, flour
and egg in a bowl and beat until
smooth. Spoon a little of the
pudding mixture over the toddler's
ramekin so that the mixture is
almost to the top of the dish.

5 Half fill three petits fours cases
with the pudding mixture.

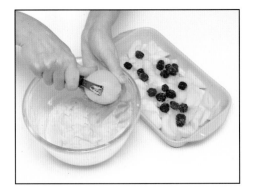

6 Grate the lemon rind and stir
with the juice into the remaining
mixture. Spoon over the large dish,
levelling the surface.

7 Put the small cakes, toddler and
adult dishes on a baking sheet
and bake in the oven for 8–10
minutes for the small cakes, 20
minutes for the ramekin and 30
minutes for the larger dish, until
they are well risen and golden
brown.

8 Dust the toddler's and adults'
portions with icing sugar and
leave to cool slightly before serving
with the custard. Warm the baby's
portion if liked and test the
temperature before serving, with the
cakes taken out of their paper cases.

TIP
If you can't get blackberries then
use raspberries instead. There's no
need to defrost before using as
they will soon thaw when added
to the hot apple.

Orange and Strawberry Shortcakes

75g/3oz/6 tbsp plain flour

50g/2oz/4 tbsp butter

25g/1oz/2 tbsp caster sugar

grated rind of ½ orange

extra sugar, for sprinkling

For the Filling

175g/6oz Greek yogurt

15ml/1 tbsp icing sugar

250g/9oz strawberries

5ml/1 tsp Cointreau (optional)

2 sprigs of fresh mint

1 Preheat the oven to 180°C/ 350°F/Gas 4. Place the flour in a bowl, cut the butter into pieces, and rub into the flour with your fingertips until the mixture resembles fine breadcrumbs.

2 Stir in the sugar and orange rind and mix to a dough.

3 Knead the dough lightly then roll out on a floured surface to 5mm/¼in thickness. Stamp out four 9cm/3½in flower shapes or fluted rounds with a biscuit cutter and 12 small car, train or other fun shapes with novelty cutters, rerolling the dough as necessary.

4 Place on a baking sheet, prick with a fork and sprinkle with a little extra sugar. Bake in the oven for 10–12 minutes until pale golden, then leave to cool on the baking sheet.

5 For the filling, blend the yogurt with the sugar and wash and hull the strawberries. Pat dry. Reserve eight of the strawberries and process or liquidize the rest. Press through a sieve and discard the seeds.

6 For the adults, put 45ml/3 tbsp of the yogurt in a bowl and stir in the Cointreau, if using. Slice four strawberries and halve two, place on a plate and cover.

7 For the toddler, slice two of the strawberries and arrange in a ring on a small plate. Spoon 30ml/2 tbsp of yogurt into the centre of the ring and serve with three of the small biscuit shapes.

8 For baby, stir 15ml/1 tbsp of the strawberry purée into the remaining natural yogurt and spoon into a small dish. Serve with one or two of the small biscuit shapes.

9 To complete the adults' portions, spoon purée over two plates to cover completely.

10 Spoon the reserved yogurt over two biscuits, add the sliced strawberries and top with the other two biscuits. Arrange on plates and decorate with halved strawberries and tiny sprigs of mint.

TIP
If you find shortbread difficult to roll out then chill for 20 minutes. Knead lightly and roll out on a surface dusted with flour, dusting the rolling pin too.

Exotic Fruit Brulée

oil, for greasing

30ml/2 tbsp demerara sugar

1 ripe mango

1 kiwi fruit

1 passion fruit

30ml/2 tbsp icing sugar

350g/12oz Greek yogurt

1 Line a baking sheet with foil then draw round the tops of two 250ml/8fl oz/1 cup ramekin dishes and one 150ml/¼ pint/⅔ cup ramekin dish. Lightly brush with oil. Sprinkle the sugar inside each marked circle in an even layer.

2 Grill the sugar discs for 2–3 minutes or until it has melted and caramelized. Leave the discs to cool on the baking sheet.

3 Slice the mango either side of the central stone and then cut six thin slices for decoration, cutting away the skin. Cut the rest of the mango flesh from the stone, removing the skin, and finely chop one quarter, dividing between the baby bowl and small ramekin. Roughly chop the remainder and divide between the larger ramekins.

4 Peel the kiwi fruit, cut in half lengthways and then slice thinly. Reserve four half slices for decoration and divide the remaining fruit among the dishes, finely chopping the fruit for baby and toddler. Cut the passion fruit in half and using a teaspoon scoop and place the seeds in the adults' dishes.

5 Stir the icing sugar into the yogurt and mix 15ml/1 tbsp into the baby's portion. Spoon 30ml/2 tbsp yogurt over the toddler's dish and level the surface with a spoon.

6 Spoon the remaining yogurt into the other two ramekins, level the surface with a spoon and chill all of them until required.

7 When ready to serve, place the larger ramekins on two plates with the reserved mango and kiwi slices arranged around the sides. Peel the sugar discs off the foil and set on top of the adult and toddler portions. Serve the brulées immediately.

TIP
Traditionally the sugar topping on a brulée is made by sprinkling demerara sugar over the top of the dessert and then grilling, or by making a caramel syrup and then pouring it over the dessert. Making the topping on oiled foil is by far the easiest and most foolproof way. Add the cooled sugar discs at the very last minute so that they stay crisp and you get that wonderful mix of crunchy sugar, velvety yogurt and refreshing fruit.

Plum Crumble

450g/1lb ripe red plums

25g/1oz/2 tbsp caster sugar

For the Topping

115g/4oz/1 cup plain flour

50g/2oz/4 tbsp butter, cut into
  pieces

25g/1oz/2 tbsp caster sugar

10ml/2 tsp chocolate dots

75g/3oz marzipan

30ml/2 tbsp rolled oats

30ml/2 tbsp flaked almonds

custard, to serve

1 Preheat the oven to 190°C/
375°F/Gas 5. Wash the plums,
cut into quarters and remove the
stones. Place in a saucepan with the
sugar and 30ml/2 tbsp water, cover
and simmer for 10 minutes.

2 Drain and spoon six plum
quarters onto a chopping board
and chop finely. Spoon the plums
into a small baby dish with a little
juice from the saucepan.

3 Drain and roughly chop six
more of the plum quarters and
place in a 150ml/¼ pint/⅔ cup
ovenproof ramekin dish with a little
of the juice from the saucepan.

4 Spoon the remaining plums into
a 750ml/1¼ pint/3⅔ cup
ovenproof dish for the adults.

5 Make the topping. Place the
flour in a bowl, rub in the butter
and then stir in the sugar.

6 Mix 45ml/3 tbsp of the crumble
mixture with the chocolate dots
then spoon over the ramekin.

7 Coarsely grate the marzipan and
stir into the remaining crumble
with the oats and almonds. Spoon
over the adults' portion.

8 Place the toddler and adult
portions on a baking sheet and
cook for 20–25 minutes until golden
brown. Leave to cool slightly before
serving. Warm baby's portion if
liked and check the temperature of
the children's food before serving.
Serve with custard.

TIP
Ovens can vary in temperature:
with fan-assisted ovens you may
need to cover the adults' dish with
foil half way through cooking to
prevent overbrowning.

Vary the fruits: cooking apples,
peaches and pears also work well.
If the plums are very sharp you
may need to add a little extra sugar.

Chocolate and Orange Trifle

½ chocolate Swiss roll

3 clementines or satsumas

20ml/4 tsp sherry

50g/2oz dark chocolate

300ml/½ pint/1¼ cups ready-made custard

90ml/6 tbsp double cream

chocolate buttons or M & M's

3 Peel the remaining clementines, roughly chop and add to the adults' bowls, sprinkling a little sherry over each.

5 Spoon 30ml/2 tbsp of the custard into a small bowl for baby and arrange on the plate with the Swiss roll and clementines. Spoon a little more custard into the ramekin and then add the rest to the adult dishes, smoothing the surface.

1 Slice the Swiss roll, halve one slice and put on a plate for baby. Put a second slice into a ramekin dish for the older child and arrange the remaining slices in two dessert bowls for the adults.

2 Peel one clementine, separate into segments and put a few on the baby plate. Chop the rest and add to the ramekin.

4 Break the chocolate into pieces and melt in a bowl over a saucepan of hot water. Stir the melted chocolate into the custard.

6 Whip the cream until it just holds its shape. Add a spoonful to the ramekin dish and two or three spoonfuls each to the adults' dishes, decorating each dish with sweets. Chill the trifles until required.

TIP
Chocolate may be melted in the microwave in a microwave-safe bowl for 2 minutes on Full Power (100%), stirring thoroughly halfway through cooking.

Some shops sell ready-made chocolate custard, buy this if available and you're short of time.

Vary the fruit depending on what is in season, sliced strawberries and orange or sliced banana and fresh or canned cherries also work well.

Apple Strudel

450g/1lb cooking apples

50g/2oz dried apricots

45ml/3 tbsp sultanas

30ml/2 tbsp soft light brown sugar

30ml/2 tbsp ground almonds

5ml/1 tsp ground cinnamon

25g/1oz/2 tbsp butter

150g/5oz/3 sheets filo pastry, defrosted if frozen

icing sugar, to dust

pouring cream, to serve

1 Preheat the oven to 200°C/ 400°F/Gas 6. Peel, core and chop the apples and place 150g/5oz in a saucepan. Chop three apricots and add to the pan with 15ml/1 tbsp sultanas, 15ml/1 tbsp sugar and 15ml/1 tbsp water. Cover and simmer for 5 minutes.

2 Chop the remaining apricots and place in a bowl with the remaining apples, sultanas, sugar, ground almonds and cinnamon. Mix together well.

3 Melt the butter in a small saucepan or microwave in a microwave-proof bowl for 30 seconds on Full Power (100%).

4 Carefully open out the pastry. Place one sheet on the work surface, brush with butter then cover with a second sheet of pastry and brush with more butter.

5 Spoon the uncooked apple mixture in a thick band along the centre of the pastry.

6 Fold the two short sides up and over the filling and brush with butter. Fold the long sides up and over the filling, opening out the pastry and folding the pastry for an attractive finish. Place on a baking sheet and brush with a little butter.

7 Brush a little of the butter over half of the third pastry sheet then fold the unbrushed half over the top to make a square. Brush again and cut into three equal strips.

8 Put a spoonful of apple at the base of each strip then fold the bottom right-hand corner up and over the filling to the left side of the strip to make a triangle.

9 Continue folding the pastry to make a triangular pasty. Repeat with the other strips.

10 Transfer to a baking sheet and brush with the remaining butter. Bake for 10 minutes, and the adults' strudel for 15 minutes, until golden and crisp. Dust with icing sugar and cool slightly.

11 Spoon the remaining cooked apple mixture into a baby dish. Mash the fruit if necessary. Transfer the toddler's portion to a plate. Slice the strudel thickly and serve with cream.

TIP
Filo pastry is usually sold frozen in 275g/10oz packs or larger. Defrost the whole pack, take out as much pastry as you need, then rewrap the rest and return to freezer.

Strawberry Pavlova

2 egg whites

115g/4oz caster sugar

2.5ml/½ tsp cornflour

2.5ml/½ tsp wine vinegar

For the Topping

150ml/¼ pint/⅔ cup double cream

250g/9oz strawberries

2 chocolate dots

green jelly sweet or little pieces
of angelica

1 Preheat the oven to 150°C/
300°F/Gas 2 and line a baking
sheet with non-stick baking paper.

2 Whisk the egg whites until stiff
and then gradually whisk in the
sugar 5ml/1 tsp at a time. Continue
whisking until smooth and glossy.

3 Blend the cornflour and vinegar
and fold into the egg whites.

4 Spoon the mixture into a large
piping bag fitted with a
medium-sized plain tube. Pipe six
small dots for baby and a snail for
the older child with a shell about
6.5cm/2½in in diameter.

5 Pipe the remaining mixture into
two 10cm/4in swirly circles and
cook in the oven for 20–25 minutes
or until firm. Lift the meringues off
the paper and leave to cool.

TIP

For perfect meringues whisk the
egg whites in a dry greasefree
bowl. Remove any trace of yolk
with a piece of shell and whisk
until the peaks are stiff but still
moist looking. Add sugar gradually
and continue whisking until very
thick. Meringues may be made
1–2 days in advance. Cover with
greaseproof paper and decorate
just before serving.

6 Whip the cream until softly
peaking and spoon over the two
large meringues and the snail,
reserving about 15ml/1 tbsp for the
baby.

7 Rinse, hull and slice the
strawberries and arrange a few
in rings over the snail. Place the snail
on a plate and add chocolate eyes and
a slice from a green jelly sweet or a
little angelica for the mouth.

8 Add some strawberries to the
adult meringues then chop or
mash a few extra slices and stir them
into the reserved cream for the baby.
Spoon into a small dish and serve
with tiny meringues.

Poached Pears

3 ripe pears

450ml/¾ pint/1⅞ cup apple juice

5ml/1 tsp powdered gelatine

few drops of green food colouring

½ small orange, rind only

½ small lemon, rind only

10ml/2 tsp chopped glacé ginger

5ml/1 tsp clear honey

5ml/1 tsp cornflour

1 red liquorice bootlace

2 small currants

1 raisin or large currant

½ glacé cherry

1 Peel the pears leaving the stalks in place. Cut a small circle out of the base of two pears and tunnel out the cores with a small knife.

2 Halve the remaining pear, discard the stalk, scoop out the core and then put them all in a pan with the apple juice. Bring to the boil, cover and simmer for 5 minutes, turning the pears once.

3 Lift out the pear halves and reserve, cooking the whole pears for a further 5 minutes or until tender. Remove with a slotted spoon and place on a serving dish reserving the cooking liquor. Finely chop one pear half and put into a small dish for baby. Reserve the other half pear for the toddler.

4 Pour half of the reserved apple juice into a bowl, place over a pan of simmering water, add the gelatine and stir until completely dissolved. Transfer to a measuring jug and pour half over the chopped pear and chill.

5 Stir a little green colouring into the remaining gelatine mixture, pour into a shallow dish or a plate with a rim for the toddler, and chill.

6 Cut away the rind from the orange and lemon and cut into thin strips. Add to the remaining apple juice with the ginger and honey and simmer over a gentle heat for 5 minutes until the rinds are soft.

7 Blend the cornflour with a little water to make a smooth paste, stir into the pan then bring the mixture to the boil and cook, stirring until thickened. Pour over the whole pears and leave to cool.

8 Place the toddler's pear, cut side down on the green jelly. To make a mouse, add a piece of red liquorice for a tail and two pieces for whiskers. Make two small cuts for eyes and tuck a currant into each slit. Add a raisin or large currant for the nose. Halve the cherry and use for ears. Serve slightly chilled with cream for the adults, if liked.

Peach Frangipane Tart

175g/6oz/1½ cups plain flour

75g/3oz/6 tbsp butter

For the Filling

50g/2oz/4 tbsp butter

50g/2oz/¼ cup caster sugar

1 egg

few drops of almond essence

50g/2oz/⅔ cup ground almonds

30ml/2 tbsp apricot jam

15ml/1 tbsp chopped candied peel

400g/14oz can peach slices in natural juice

15ml/1 tbsp flaked almonds

15ml/1 tbsp fromage frais or natural yogurt

icing sugar, for dusting

crème fraîche or natural yogurt, to serve

1 Place the flour in a bowl, cut the butter into small pieces and rub into the flour with your fingertips until the mixture resembles fine breadcrumbs.

2 Stir in 30–35ml/6–7 tsp water and mix to a smooth dough. Knead lightly on a floured surface and roll out thinly.

3 Lift the pastry over a rolling pin and use to line an 18cm/7in flan dish pressing down against the sides of the dish. Trim the top.

4 Reroll the trimmings and cut out twelve 5cm/2in circles with a fluted biscuit cutter, pressing into sections of a mini muffin tin. Chill the pastry for 15 minutes.

5 Preheat the oven to 190°C/ 375°F/Gas 5. Line the large flan dish with greaseproof paper and fill with baking beans. Cook for 10 minutes then remove the baking beans and paper and cook the shell for a further 5 minutes.

6 Meanwhile make the filling: cream together the butter and sugar in a bowl until light and fluffy. Beat the eggs and almond essence together then gradually beat into the creamed sugar. Stir in the ground almonds and set aside.

7 Divide the jam among the small and large tarts, spread it into a thin layer in the large tart and sprinkle with candied peel. Spoon all of the almond mixture over the top and level the surface.

8 Drain the peaches and set aside three slices for baby. Cut three slices into chunky pieces and divide among six of the small tarts, leaving six with just jam.

9 Arrange the remaining peaches over the top of the large tart and sprinkle with flaked almonds.

10 Cook the small tarts for 10 minutes and the large tart for 25 minutes until the filling is set and browned. Dust the large tart with icing sugar and leave to cool slightly.

11 Purée the reserved peaches for baby in a processor or liquidizer. Mix with fromage frais or yogurt and spoon into a small dish. Serve with two plain jam tarts.

12 Arrange a few fruity jam tarts on a plate for the toddler. Cut the large tart into wedges and serve with crème fraîche or natural yogurt for the adults. Test the temperature of the children's tarts before serving.

Honey and Summer Fruit Mousse

10ml/2 tsp powdered gelatine

500g/1¼lb bag frozen summer fruits, defrosted

20ml/4 tsp caster sugar

500g/1¼lb tub fromage frais or Greek yogurt

150ml/¼ pint/⅔ cup whipping cream

25ml/5 tsp clear honey

1 Put 30ml/2 tbsp cold water in a cup and sprinkle the gelatine over making sure that all grains of gelatine have been absorbed. Soak for 5 minutes, then heat in a saucepan of simmering water until the gelatine dissolves and the liquid is clear. Cool slightly.

2 For baby, process or liquidize 50g/2oz of fruit to a purée and stir in 5ml/1 tsp sugar. Mix 45ml/3 tbsp fromage frais or yogurt with 5ml/1 tsp sugar in a separate bowl.

3 Put alternate spoonfuls of fromage frais or yogurt and purée into a small dish for baby. Swirl the mixtures together with a teaspoon. Chill until required.

4 For the toddler, process 50g/2oz fruit with 5ml/1 tsp sugar. Mix 60ml/4 tbsp fromage frais or yogurt with 5ml/1 tsp sugar then stir in 10ml/2 tsp fruit purée.

5 Stir 5ml/1 tsp gelatine into the fruit purée and 5ml/1 tsp into the fromage frais or yogurt mixture. Spoon the fruit mixture into the base of a perspex beaker or glass and chill until set.

6 For the adults, whip the cream until softly peaking. Fold in the remaining fromage frais or yogurt and honey and add the remaining gelatine. Pour into two, 250ml/8fl oz/1 cup moulds. Chill until set.

7 Spoon the remaining fromage frais mixture over the set fruit layer in the serving glass for the toddler and chill until set.

8 To serve, dip one of the dishes for the adults in hot water, count to 15, then loosen the edges with your fingertips, invert on to a large plate and, holding mould and plate together, jerk to release the mousse and remove mould. Repeat with the other mould. Spoon the remaining fruits and some juice around the desserts and serve.

TIP
If you have a small novelty mould you may prefer to set the toddler's portion in this rather than a glass or plastic container.

Make sure the gelatine isn't too hot before adding to fromage frais or yogurt or it may curdle.

Hot Fruit Salad with Ginger Cream

2 oranges

4 bananas

50g/2oz stoned dates

30ml/2 tbsp sultanas

25g/1oz/2 tbsp butter

45ml/3 tbsp demerara sugar

30ml/2 tbsp Cointreau or brandy

vanilla ice cream, to serve

For the Ginger Cream

150ml/¼ pint/⅔ cup double cream

15ml/1 tbsp chopped glacé ginger

grated rind of 1 orange

3 Peel and slice the bananas. Roughly chop the dates. Arrange a few orange segments, slices of banana, pieces of date and a few sultanas on a plate for the baby.

5 Stir the Cointreau or brandy into the pan, bring to the boil then quickly light with a match. Spoon the fruit into a serving bowl as soon as the flames subside. Serve the adults' flambéed fruit with ginger cream and the toddler's portion with ice cream. Test the temperature of toddler's portion before serving.

1 First make the ginger cream: whip the cream until it just holds its shape, then finely chop the ginger and stir into the cream with the orange rind. Spoon into a small serving dish.

4 Melt the butter in a frying pan, add the remaining fruit and fry for 2 minutes, then stir in the sugar and cook for 2 minutes, until lightly browned. Spoon a few pieces of fruit into a bowl for the toddler.

TIP

Flaming dishes look so spectacular but are really very easy to do. The secret is to add the spirit to hot liquid, bring the liquid back to the boil then quickly light it with a match and stand back. The flames will subside in a minute or two. But if you are at all worried they can be quickly extinguished by covering the pan with a lid or baking sheet.

2 Cut a slice off the top and bottom of each orange and cut the remaining peel and pith away in slices. Cut into segments.

INDEX